CANADIAN BAND MUSIC

A Qualitative Guide to Canadian Composers and Their Works for Band

MICHAEL BURCH-PESSES

Published by
Meredith Music Publications
a division of G.W. Music, Inc.
4899 Lerch Creek Ct., Galesville, MD 20765
http://www.meredithmusic.com

ISBN-13: 978 1-57463-087-9
Library of Congress Control Number: 2007942089
Printed and bound in U.S.A.

Contents

Foreword

It is a credit to the author that the repertoire he highlights in this book is finally getting the attention it merits. It is ironic, yet strangely appropriate, that it took an American to "discover" this body of Canadian music.

Canadians as a people are still charting their psychological course away from a colonial past, as part of the British Commonwealth, towards completely embracing their country's more recent role as a full-status player in the international community. The national inferiority complex that went with being a dominion of the United Kingdom routinely manifested itself in the unquestioning acceptance of foreign artists and cultural imports in Canada (e.g., music, films, television programming) as being automatically superior to homegrown artists and products, with the result that, to this day, too little Canadian music is known and appreciated, even in Canada, though the situation is slowly improving. Put differently not long ago by the now-deceased Ottawa arts *doyenne*, Trudi LeCaine, "Canadian artists have for too long hidden their light under a bushel."

In an article entitled "About Canadian Music: The PR failure," published almost forty years ago in *Musicanada* magazine, the composer-author-educator, John Beckwith, articulated the need for Canadians to publicize the existence of their own music. But until this moment, early in the twenty-first century, there has existed no comprehensive catalogue of Canadian band music, no annotated listing to which conductors could refer when searching for likely material to include in concert or competition programming. Since much of this repertoire is unpublished, a significant portion of it is generally unknown and unplayed even in Canada. The true significance of that can only be appreciated by considering the number of instrumental (especially wind) music programs in elementary, middle, and secondary schools across the country, and all the college, university, civic, and military bands and wind ensembles that exist from coast to coast in Canada. Their concert programs year-in and year-out feature an overwhelming percentage of non-Canadian music, and a significant opportunity on behalf of Canadian culture is being lost.

This long overdue book identifies the contemporary Canadian band repertoire and gives conductors the practical information they need about each piece to enable and encourage them to make informed choices in programming. It also demonstrates through discussion and analysis that the Canadian repertoire for concerted winds is dynamic and evolving, as rich and varied and full of craft and inventiveness as any that exists elsewhere for the medium of the wind band. There are many wonderful discoveries to be made in the pages of this book. I wish you pleasant reading and happy music making!

S. Timothy Maloney
Editor, *Canadian Winds / Vents canadiens*
March, 2007

FOREWORD

MICHAEL BURCH-PESSES TAKES US on a fascinating expedition to the North, a trip of discovery in which old favorites are rediscovered and new favorites are uncovered. This insightful and informative study contains a brief biography on each composer (including birth and death dates) and a detailed account of each work. Each description also lists the difficulty, duration, date of composition and availability. The result is a rich and varied compendium of wind band works that have been neglected or undiscovered.

This easy-to-use collection brings to light many works that have been veiled in obscurity. I highly recommend it to anyone seeking programming ideas for wind band. It should be of interest to anyone passionate about discovering new repertoire and excited by the quest to uncover many hidden treasures.

Jim Cochran
President, Shattinger Music

Acknowledgements

Shortly after I began my college teaching career in Oregon I began to receive invitations to conduct and adjudicate at music festivals in Canada. Those invitations have resulted in the most wonderful and rewarding friendships with countless Canadian band directors from British Columbia to Ontario. As I began to research this book I quickly learned how generous my Canadian colleagues could be with their time, advice, and words of encouragement. Without their help this book would not have been possible.

The first of these colleagues was Marko Rnic, Head of Music and Director of Bands at St. George's School in Vancouver, British Columbia. Marko directed me to the Canadian Music Centre, a vital resource in my research. He not only encouraged me as I progressed through this project, but also introduced me to some of the finer eating establishments in Vancouver. It's astonishing how much weight one can gain while doing research.

The Canadian Music Centre itself could not have been more welcoming or helpful. Colin Miles and his staff in Vancouver, and Jason van Eyk and his staff in Toronto were much more than gracious as I pored through their scores and mined their powerful database.

I am especially grateful to Howard Cable, incomparable icon of Canadian music and peerless raconteur, who spent an entire afternoon regaling me with stories of his remarkable career and enlightening me about some of the history of band music in Canada. I never knew I could laugh so much and learn so much all at the same time.

I must thank all the composers listed here, almost all of whom devoted generous amounts of time to communicating with me, both verbally and in writing. Composers are seldom reluctant to talk about their work, and their willingness to assist me has resulted, I believe, in program notes that are both illuminating and interesting.

I am greatly indebted to my four Canadian colleagues who volunteered to read my draft and offer their recommendations. The first is the indefatigable David Marlatt, whom I met at the Midwest Clinic. An accomplished composer, arranger, performer, and businessman, David exemplifies all that is good about Canadian music in the 21st century. The second is Gillian MacKay, conductor and music educator at the University or Toronto, who presented the most fascinating workshop on conducting and mime at the Oregon Music Educators Conference in January 2006. I now refer to her as my favorite mime. (Please don't tell her she's the only mime I know.)

Gillian's colleague at the University of Toronto, Jeffrey Reynolds, is the most delightful and understated gentleman, and was the first to offer to proofread my draft. I am immensely grateful for his initiative and generosity. Last, but by no means least, is Keith Kinder, Director of Bands at McMaster University in

Hamilton, Ontario. A well-known and highly respected researcher and lover of band lore, Keith was unstinting in sharing from his storehouse of knowledge.

Finally, I owe my profound gratitude to my loving wife, Jane, without whose gentle and constant encouragement I would have been completely at sea. I can't imagine how much more difficult this book would have been without her at my side. Friend, editor, cheerleader, president of my fan club and much more, she is the helpmate on whom I can always rely, and the inextinguishable light toward which I can always turn.

INTRODUCTION

MY LOVE FOR AND interest in Canada began long before I ever imagined I might write about Canadian composers and their works for band. In November 1979, during my career as a bandmaster in the U.S. Navy, the world was electrified by the news that the U.S. embassy in Tehran, Iran had been seized and its diplomats taken hostage by Iranians. The "Iranian hostage crisis" led the news headlines for more than a year as our nation worried about the 52 hostages, concerned that we might never see them alive again.

The hostages were released at last in January 1981, 444 days after the fall of the embassy, and everyone in America breathed a sigh of relief. It wasn't until after their release that we learned many American diplomats had evaded capture and were given refuge by members of the Canadian embassy. At no small risk to themselves, our Canadian friends unhesitatingly had sheltered and cared for our diplomats, making sure not to arouse the Iranians' suspicions by suddenly getting rid of more trash or having more dirty laundry than usual. They even arranged for a small cadre of diplomats to be issued Canadian passports so they might return to the U.S. and provide intelligence regarding the situation at the American embassy. For more than a year they cared for their American friends and made sure they returned home safely.

From the moment I learned of the risks that our neighbors to the north took on our behalf, I have been an unabashed fan of Canada and Canadians. Although I still don't quite understand hockey, I do understand the courage and daring required to take such bold steps with little apparent concern for the possible consequences. I have had numerous occasions to visit Canada and have told this story many times, but even now, after more than two decades have passed, it is difficult to explain how profoundly the actions of our brave friends affected me. Our two countries don't always see things eye to eye, but I like to think America would just as unhesitatingly return that remarkable favor if the situation ever arose. Let us hope it never does.

The book itself came about as a result of an invitation I received to adjudicate the senior bands at the week long Alberta Band Festival at Red Deer College in Edmonton, Alberta. Alberta's high school and community bands, most of which perform at the festival, may choose to play a "Canadian" work; that is, a piece by a Canadian composer. As the week progressed, I discovered that I had never before heard any of these beautiful Canadian band pieces. Up to that time I had considered myself fairly well versed in band literature.

It is fair to say that a high proportion of this music was based on Canadian folk songs. Despite my chagrin at my unfamiliarity with these pieces, I was quite taken with them. Their beauty and simple elegance appealed to me quite strongly, largely because of their melodic charm and professional scoring. I've always been fond of American folk songs, whose melodies are often very simple and at the same time very touching, and whose lyrics range from the historic to the comic to the tragic. As the festival progressed I began to feel that I wasn't just visiting another country, but had entered another world where the band literature was unknown to me. When I returned home it struck me that if I didn't know this literature, most of my American colleagues probably didn't either. Wouldn't it be wonderful, I thought to myself, if there were some sort of literature list of quality Canadian music?

Several years later, when I became eligible for a sabbatical, I decided to act on that thought. What you hold in your hands is the result of my sabbatical research, a compilation of quality band works from grade 1 through grade 6 by Canadian composers. It is my hope that this listing will entice you to obtain and perform this fine literature regardless of your nationality. When I began my sabbatical I had no idea I would have such a good time conducting research instead of a band. I feared that trying to find information about Canadian wind literature would be tedious and frustrating, but the exact opposite was true. I had many resources from which to draw, and learning about each new work was like uncovering a nugget in a gold mine.

The John Adaskin Project

In undertaking my research I was able to follow the example of the John Adaskin Project, a joint venture of the Canadian Music Educators Association and the Canadian Music Centre (CMC). Stretching from the 1960's to the 1980's, the John Adaskin Project sought to acquaint music educators with suitable Canadian repertoire, promote publication of additional repertoire, and encourage composers to add to the repertoire. From the John Adaskin Project came two very helpful books by Patricia Martin Shand of the University of Toronto: *Canadian Music: A Selective Guidelist for Teachers* (1978), and *Guidelist of Unpublished Canadian Band Music* (1987). Most of the band works in those two publications are listed and expanded upon here.

The Canadian Music Centre

Many of these works, and the two books by Professor Shand, are available through the Canadian Music Centre (CMC), a remarkable non-profit organization dedicated to supporting and promoting Canadian music of all types. Formed in 1959, the mission of the Centre is to promote the music of its Associate Composers, to encourage the performance and appreciation of Canadian music, and to make it available throughout Canada and around the world. With offices in five provinces and a powerful web site, the CMC fills a great need by loaning the unpublished music of its Associate Composers *at virtually no cost* to those who wish to obtain and perform it. Please see "How to Use This Book" for more information about obtaining music from the CMC.

Canadian Music Publishers and Composers

This may cause you to ask, "Why is there so much unpublished Canadian music?" Part of the reason is that music publishers are almost nonexistent in

Canada. Certainly a few Canadian composers, such as Michael Colgrass, Andre Jutras, Jim Duff, and Douglas Court, have been published by American publishing houses, but the great majority either have had difficulty in finding publishers, have not sought them out, or simply have decided to self-publish or make their works available through the CMC. At this writing there is only one major music publisher in Canada, Eighth Note Publications, that actively publicizes, markets, and distributes its music. This resource guide lists only a small fraction of the works in the Eighth Note Publications catalog, and I encourage you examine it on line in greater detail at www.enpmusic.com.

One example of quality Canadian music virtually unknown outside Canada is the music commissioned by the Northdale Concert Band, an excellent community band. In 1986 the Northdale Concert Band, recognizing the lack of Canadian band music for formal events, decided to embark on what they called the Canada Band Project. The band commissioned six well known and highly respected Canadian composers to write new works for the band to perform. The works were to be appropriate for national and heritage events, where a band might be called on to play music suitable for such festive occasions. They also were intended to be melodic, festive, accessible music for official proceedings such as graduations, inaugural events, and other official functions.

The Northdale Concert Band performed the world premieres of each of the first six commissions at Expo '86 in Vancouver, B.C. on Canada Day, July 1, to mark the International Year of Canadian Music. The response to the music was so positive that the band took the project one step further by publishing all the works in the collection and offering them for sale under the imprint, "Northdale Music Press Limited." Virtually every composer involved in the Canada Band Project is listed in this book, including Howard Cable, Donald Coakley, and more.

Most of us have never heard of the Canada Band Project because the Northdale Concert Band and its offshoot, Northdale Music Press Limited, are volunteer organizations that distribute their publications themselves because they would lose money if they used a distributor. Their publications are available only through their website. All the works in this book are worthy of your consideration, but I particularly encourage you to explore the quality offerings of Northdale Music Press Limited at www.northdalemusic.com.

In seeking out the latest information on each entry, I was most fortunate to be able to speak directly with many of the composers. Without exception, the composers with whom I talked were delighted to discuss their musical children. At the same time, some expressed regret that their compositions had not been more widely performed. One such composer, now retired from his teaching career but still writing music regularly, talked about one of his band pieces that has suffered from what he called "premiere-itis." Aside from its premiere, it has never been performed, despite its initial positive reviews.

The Canadian Wind Band Repertoire Project

The Canadian Band Association, recognizing the fact that so many worthy band works have gone unnoticed, has embarked on The Canadian Wind Band Repertoire Project. Through this project, the Association has set out to improve the awareness, appreciation, performance and general condition of Canadian wind band repertoire. The ultimate goal is to establish a series of print, audio and online resources designed for use by educators, band directors and wind band enthusiasts across Canada and around the world. The core challenge of the Project is to create a publicly accessible, web-based database of Canadian-based repertoire containing the following:

1) An annotated list of wind band music written by Canadians
2) A growing number of review/study guides; and
3) An audio recording of each listed work. Eventually these resources will be available in book, CD, and electronic formats.

Ultimately, the Project will support Canadian composers directly by commissioning new works at all levels of musical challenge. What a powerful resource this ongoing project will be!

Recordings of Canadian Band Music

Reference recordings of quality band works seem to be growing in importance. The recordings that accompany the *Teaching Music Through Performance in Band* series, for example, allow the director to listen to high quality recordings of the works they are considering before actually purchasing the music. I appreciate the fact that directors may be reluctant to spend their limited budget on music they have never heard, and the ready availability of CD recordings of music published by American music publishers makes the decision about what music to buy much easier. By contrast, relatively few of the listings here are paired with a recording, but I hope this won't discourage the reader from obtaining and performing these fine works. I have listed all recordings I was able to locate, and I encourage the reader to be bold and adventurous when considering a Canadian work that doesn't have a reference recording. **All works available through the CMC are free to the requestor (the only cost is return shipping), so the financial risk is low and the value will be high.** I also encourage any director who is considering programming one of these works that doesn't list a reference recording to contact me. By the time I receive your message I may have located a recording of the work you are considering. I realize this could result in countless messages, but that would be a delightful problem to have. I would be happy to correspond with anyone who is interested in this wonderful music.

Historical Notes of Interest

It is certainly worth mentioning that my research uncovered other significant contributions to the world of music by Canadians other than those listed herein. Among the most significant of these revelations is the fact that three of the nine charter members of the American Bandmasters Association (ABA) were bandmasters from Canada. In addition to Americans Edwin Franko Goldman of New York; LT Charles Benter, Director of the United States Navy Band in Washington, D. C.; Victor J. Grabel, Conductor of the Chicago Concert Band; Albert Austin Harding, Director of Bands at the University of Illinois; Arthur Pryor, Director of Arthur Pryor's Band, New York, NY; and Frank Simon, Director of the ARMCO Band, Middletown, Ohio, the list included Canadians J. J. Gagnier, Director of His Majesty's Grenadier Guards Band, Montreal, Canada; Richard B. Hayward, Director of the Toronto Concert Band, Toronto, Canada; and Charles O'Neill, Director of the Royal 22nd Regiment Band, Quebec, Canada. Given the significance of the ABA in shaping the modern concert band, expanding its repertoire, and championing a high quality music education for its conductors, Canada may justly be proud of its role in this important work.

Additionally, I discovered that L. P. Laurendeau, the arranger of so many early works for concert band that I played in my formative years, was also a Canadian. Louis-Phillippe Laurendeau was born in 1861 in St. Hyacinthe, Quebec, and became one of the most important and prolific composers and arrangers of music for Carl Fischer. At one point approximately 25 percent of Carl Fischer's band and orchestra catalog was either composed or arranged by Laurendeau. He lived in Canada most of his life, and died far too soon at the age of fifty-five. Readers who, like me, have seen his name in the upper right hand corner of so many fine transcriptions for band, will appreciate knowing that a Montreal street was named after him in 1931.

Mea Culpa

Of course, this book will be out of date by the time you read it. Composers in Canada continue to write new works for band whether they are published or not, and the Canadian Music Centre continues to accept music from its Associate Composers and make it available to those who request it. There also remains the very real possibility that I may have omitted some valuable works even though numerous Canadian colleagues were remarkably generous with their time and assistance in vetting my findings. The responsibility for such omissions or any other error is mine.

This resource guide is intended not just to help non-Canadian band directors explore a wealth of quality music from Canada, perhaps as they set about programming a concert with an international theme. It also provides Canadian directors with a list of literature that reflects their remarkably scenic, historic, and diverse nation. Regardless of the nationality of the reader, I wish you good fortune and good music as you leaf through these pages.

Michael Burch-Pesses
burchpem@aol.com
Fall, 2007

How To Use This Book—
Your Guide to Northern Delights

1. If you are looking for works of quality by a specific composer:

The entries in this book are alphabetical by composer, then alphabetical by title of composition. Index 1 is a quick reference guide to the composers in this book.

2. If you are looking for quality works at a specific grade level:

I have included works of quality in every grade, and Index 2 is the complete list of works by grade.

3. Explanation of entries:

The listing for each work includes a program note and information on how to obtain that work, whether through a publisher, the composer, or the Canadian Music Centre. I have engaged in almost no creative writing with regard to composers' biographies or program notes. I have edited biographies and program notes only for brevity, clarity, and consistency, and to conform to my U.S. publisher's style guide. Each biography and program note lists the source or sources for that information.

4. Special note for teachers:

Appendix 1 includes suggestions for four year plans for programming Canadian band literature at each grade level. This appendix is intended to spark your own creativity.

5. **Don't miss this:**

The Canadian Music Centre (CMC) is a nationwide non-profit institution that archives and promotes the work of its associate composers. To become an Associate Composer of the CMC one must take part in a juried competition. Once the CMC board accepts the jury's positive recommendations the composers are accepted as Associate Composers. This vetting process helps to ensure that works held by the CMC are works of quality by composers of note.

Compositions held at the various offices of the CMC (there are five offices throughout the provinces) are available for **free loan** to anyone in the world for up to 90 days. (Yes, American band directors, this includes you!) All you need do is pay the postage to return the work to the CMC, and include the information about the performance of the work that you have available, such as a copy of the printed program, and/or a poster advertising the concert, etc.

Most works in manuscript, some of the published music, recordings, and books may also be purchased from the CMC. The CMC catalog is online at their website, www.musiccentre.ca, where you may search by title or composer on their database.

The CMC is recognized throughout the world for the services it provides. As a non-profit organization they would be pleased to accept tax-deductible charitable donations.

Murray Adaskin (1906–2002)

Dr. Murray Adaskin was a member of a distinguished Canadian family that included Gordon Adaskin, painter; musician brothers John and Harry Adaskin; and his wife, Frances James, soprano. He enjoyed a distinguished and varied career that spanned most of the twentieth century.

Born in Toronto, where he started his musical studies, Adaskin continued his studies in New York and Paris. Violinist for ten years with the Toronto Symphony, Adaskin also studied composition with John Weinzweig, Charles Jones and Darius Milhaud.

Adaskin was appointed Head of the Department of Music at the University of Saskatchewan from 1952 to 1966, after which he became Composer-in-Residence. This was the first position of its type at a Canadian university. Dr. Adaskin helped make Saskatoon a major center for the performance of contemporary Canadian music by conducting the Saskatoon Symphony for five years, commissioning new works and organizing concerts of Canadian music. He was appointed to the Canada Council from 1966–1969, and in 1980 was made an Officer of the Order of Canada, one of Canada's highest civilian honors, in recognition of a lifetime of achievement and merit in service to Canada. He retired to Victoria in 1973, where he composed more than half his works.

His music is generally lyrical, clearly crafted and rhythmically vital, and has been widely performed, broadcast, recorded and admired since the 1950's. He was an influential and charismatic teacher: thousands of students took his music appreciation classes in Saskatchewan and Victoria. His involvement with the cultural life of his community and country took many forms: composing pieces for young musicians and for special occasions; organizing concerts and festivals; and adjudicating competitions. In recognition of his many achievements he received six honorary doctorates. Adaskin was a mentor and good friend to five generations of Canadian musicians, many of whom consider him to be one of Canada's most important and generous musicians. (CMC, Contemporary Canadian Composers, Order of Canada, and Rodney Sharman)

Night Is No Longer Summer Soft
Difficulty: Grade 4
Duration: 2:50
Composed in 1970
Available through CMC (www.musiccentre.ca)

Commissioned by The Music Teachers' Association of Saskatoon Schools, this tonal work is based on interlocking melodic and rhythmic motives that are artistically developed and extended. Motives are short and there are frequent intervallic leaps. The tempo is slow and the meter predominantly 4/4 with some changes to 3/4, and the composer indicates that the character of the piece is "somber and gloomy." This is an excellent piece to develop dexterity, intonation, dynamic contrast, and rhythmic precision. (CMC and Patricia Shand)

A pedagogical discussion of this work can be found on page 37 of *Guidelist of Unpublished Canadian Band Music Suitable for Student Performers* by Patricia Martin Shand.

LOUIS APPLEBAUM (1918–2000)

COMPOSER, CONDUCTOR AND ARTS administrator, Louis Applebaum was intimately connected with music in Canada. He was instrumental in the formation and administration of many national arts institutions—the Canada Council, the Canadian League of Composers, the Canadian Music Centre and the National Arts Center. He helped focus the direction of culture in Canada, including chairing the Federal Cultural Policy Review Committee, a nationwide consultation on cultural concerns.

Applebaum composed hundreds of scores: for film producers in Canada, Hollywood and New York; for the National Film Board; for radio, television, theater, orchestra, band, and smaller ensembles. His many awards included the Canadian Film Award, the Wilderness and Anik Awards, as well as an Academy Award nomination for the score to "The Story of G.I. Joe." He was made a Companion of the Order of Canada, Canada's highest civilian award, in recognition of his leadership in furthering the development of music in Canada as a composer, conductor, and administrator.

Applebaum was widely known in association with the Stratford Festival of Canada, North America's largest classical repertory theater, both as music director and composer since its inception. He established the music program there and provided incidental music for festival productions. His career as a composer and his remarkably extensive range of commissions, together with his energetic administrative leadership, established Applebaum as one of the most prolific and accomplished musicians in Canada. (CMC, The Canadian Encyclopedia, and Order of Canada)

Glorious 100th
Difficulty: Grade 5
Duration: 1:15
Published 1994 by Northdale Music Press (www.northdalemusic.com)

Glorious 100th, a fanfare for brass and percussion, was first played to launch the gala celebrations commemorating the 100th anniversary of Massey Hall, a venerable Toronto landmark in the Canadian musical scene. Commissioned by The Founders' Fund of the Corporation of Massey Hall/Roy Thomson Hall, *Glorious 100th* was performed at the June 14, 1994, gala evening by the brass and percussion players of the Toronto Symphony under the direction of Victor Feldbrill.

Massey Hall, affectionately known as "The Grand Old Lady of Shuter Street," has been acclaimed as one of the best concert halls in the world. It is the original home of the Toronto Symphony Orchestra and the Toronto Mendelssohn Choir (which first performed there in 1895), and over the years has been the site of concerts by a wide range of performers in a variety of styles—from orchestras and opera companies to small ensembles and soloists, from classical through jazz to rock, including the famous concert in May 15, 1953, featuring Charlie Parker, Dizzy Gillespie, Bud Powell, Charlie Mingus and Max Roach. (Jeffrey Reynolds and Northdale Music Press, used by permission)

High Spirits
Difficulty: Grade 5
Duration: 6:00
Published 2007 by Northdale Music Press (www.northdalemusic.com)

High Spirits was commissioned for "The Canada Band Project" by the Northdale Concert Band through the Ontario Arts Council. In response to the lack of Canadian band music for special occasions, the band commissioned six of Canada's most accomplished composers to create works for Northdale to perform. On Canada Day, July 1, 1986, the band performed the world premiere of the entire collection at Expo '86. *High Spirits*, subtitled, "A short overture for concert band," is an excellent opening work that can be performed by some middle school bands and most high school bands. It existed for some time in manuscript form and was performed regularly after its premiere. This new edition makes Applebaum's excellent work available again in an easily readable format. (© Northdale Music Press, used by permission)

Passacaglia and Toccata
Difficulty: Grade 5
Duration: 7:35
Composed in 1986
Available through CMC (www.musiccentre.ca)

This work was commissioned by Wilfrid Laurier University through the Ontario Arts Council and at the request of Michael Purves-Smith, the conductor of the wind ensemble at Wilfrid Laurier University in Waterloo, Ontario. As a specialist in baroque instruments, he had performed in the past in the theatre orchestra at the Stratford Festival, with which the composer had a long-lived association. Professor Purves-Smith also conducts the Wellington Winds, whose CD "An Artist's Neighborhood" is a valuable source of contemporary Canadian repertoire.

The Passacaglia (4:15) is introduced by a sort of cheerleader call, which returns in a different guise later in the movement. The ground bass of the passacaglia provides opportunities for interjections by various combinations of upper-register instruments. An interlude in this format is introduced quietly by the clarinet family. The beginning tempo is quarter note = 96–100, and slows to quarter note = 88.

The Toccata (3:20) recalls the sports stadium when a straightforward sports march interrupts the rhythmic thrust of this movement. The contrasting dynamics and rhythms that surround the sports march should encourage the players to enjoy the performance. The tempo is quarter note = 120 throughout, with mixed meter providing a technical challenge. (CMC and Michael Purves-Smith)

Suite of Miniature Dances
Difficulty: Grade 5
Duration: 5:00
Published 1986 by Northdale Music Press (www.northdalemusic.com)

This superb work resulted from Applebaum's role as music director for the world-famous Stratford Shakespearean Festival in Stratford, Ontario. The challenging set of dances, notable for its Neoclassical style, transparent textures and mixed meters, is one of the composer's most highly regarded works.

Suite of Miniature Dances is drawn from the incidental music for a ballroom scene in the Stratford Festival's production of Shakespeare's *All's Well That Ends Well.* That scene (Act II, scene iii) required a set of dances that had to be distinctive since they identified specific characters, and brief so they would not disturb the dramatic flow. Each of the eight movements is named for a dance form of the 16th century: *1. Promenade – 2. Coranto – 3. Gavotte – 4. Promenade II – 5. Gigue – 6. Sarabande – 7. Menuet – 8. Valse.*

The premiere performance, held in 1953 during the inaugural season of the world-renowned Stratford Festival in Stratford, Ontario, was directed by Tyrone Guthrie and starred Alec Guinness and Irene Worth. Although the 1953 production used a seven-player pit orchestra of winds and harp, it has been re-orchestrated for full concert band. (CMC, Keith Kinder, Michael Purves-Smith, and Northdale Music Press, used by permission)

The suite has been recorded by the University of Calgary Wind Ensemble on a CD entitled *from the mountains rising* (Unical UC-CD9503).

A pedagogical discussion of this work can be found on page 103 of *Canadian Music: A Selective Guidelist for Teachers* by Patricia Martin Shand.

Three Stratford Fanfares
Difficulty: Grade 5
Duration: 2:00
Published 1993 by Northdale Music Press (www.northdalemusic.com)

Three Stratford Fanfares, written for the 1953 opening season of the Stratford Festival, has been intimately associated with the now world-renowned Shakespearean festival ever since. It was first published in 1966 by Leeds Music (Canada) Limited (eventually MCI) but went out of print. Louis Applebaum reacquired the copyright and assigned it to Northdale for release of its edition.

The Festival opened in a huge tent with Tyrone Guthrie's productions of *Richard III* and *All's Well that Ends Well. Richard III*, which describes several battles and pompous court scenes, calls for many "tuckets, alarums and fanfares" requiring brass players in the orchestral ensemble that provides the incidental music. In this production, a small brass and percussion group served as the "pit orchestra"—the pit being a small boxed-in area at one corner of Stratford's thrust stage.

Since the musicians were then in a tent, there was a question as to how best to warn the audience that the performance was about to begin or that the intermission was over. Buzzers and recorded announcements seemed inappropriate. Because a brass group was available, it was suggested that a fanfare, played live, could serve that purpose. Thus began a tradition that continues to this day: at each performance in the now permanent Festival Theatre, a small brass group (most often a quartet of fanfare trumpets and a field drum) plays a fanfare in four different locations within and outside the theatre, to call the audience to their seats.

During its 50 years, the Stratford season has grown to nine months of operation. With eight performances a week, these fanfares have so far received about 100,000 performances. They are widely used and recognized as the signature tune of the Stratford Festival on radio and television. (© Northdale Music Press, used by permission)

MICHAEL CONWAY BAKER (B. 1937)

THE SON OF VAUDEVILLE and radio comedian Phil Baker, Michael Conway Baker was born in West Palm Beach, Florida. He had a nomadic childhood and attended 13 schools in 12 years in the United States and Canada. With the help of a record collection and later a piano, he taught himself the basics of musical theory. He began formal piano studies in Vancouver, his mother's hometown. He was admitted to the London College of Music, and went on to study composition at the University of British Columbia with Jean Coulthard and Elliot Weisgarber. Baker holds three degrees: Associate of the London College of Music (1959); Bachelor of Music, University of British Columbia (1966); and Master of Arts, Western Washington University (1971).

While other composers in the 1960's used chance or mathematical formulas to write music, Baker used the concepts of melody, harmony and form. He brought a contemporary approach to classical ideas, and the result is music that is both accessible and original.

Baker's music is characterized by strong emotional expression of a predominantly tonal and lyrical nature. He characterizes his serious music as essentially tonal music that reflects traditional elements of the past while using 20th century techniques and approaches. His abundant melodies, rich harmonies and expert orchestration make an immediate appeal, and his use of traditional forms shows a wealth of invention in familiar frameworks. He rarely uses key signatures because of his music's constantly shifting tonal centers. His music is often of an evocative nature and lends itself to extramusical venues such as dance, skating and film. He stresses his philosophy that convincing music can only come from true conviction and he urges young composers to follow their personal muse and not the dictates of others.

Much of Baker's most highly-acclaimed music has been for films, such as "The Grey Fox," "One Magic Christmas," and "John and the Missus." Baker and his music were also an integral part of Expo '86 in Vancouver. His Fanfare to Expo 86 opened the proceedings, and he produced scores for the films "Discovery" for the British Columbia Pavilion; "Island in Space" for the United Nations Pavilion (which was also used for Expo 88 in Australia); and "The Emerging North" for the Northwest Territories Pavilion. As well as the JUNO for Best Classical Composition, Baker has been nominated for eleven film awards and has received six, including three Genies and an ACTRA award.

He is a recipient of the Order of British Columbia, an award given to recognize those who have served with the greatest distinction and excelled in any field of endeavor to benefit the people of the Province or elsewhere. The Order represents the highest form of recognition the Province can extend to its citizens. (CMC, The Canadian Encyclopedia, New Grove Dictionary of Music and Musicians, and www.michaelconwaybaker.com.)

Chanson Joyeuse
Difficulty: Grade 5
Duration: 7:00
Composed in 1989
Available through CMC (www.musiccentre.ca)

In 1987 the CBC commissioned five short "festive" orchestral pieces to be performed by the Vancouver Symphony during the Christmas season. Baker's contribution was *Chanson Joyeuse, op. 78*. In 1989, after many requests, he arranged the work for band, with the premiere performed by the University of British Columbia Concert Band, Martin Berinbaum conducting.

The composer wanted to write a "catchy" tune that would attract the audience. The piece uses a lovely lyrical melody that is given rhythmic momentum by a 3+3+2 note grouping. Although the score indicates that this version was intended for school bands, Baker made no compromises for young players. The first statement of the tune is written for E-flat clarinet with no doubling, and the clarinets and saxophones have extended soli sections with many cross rhythms. (CMC, Keith Kinder, and Michael Conway Baker)

March Mechanique
Difficulty: Grade 3
Duration: 2:00
Composed in 2002
Available through CMC and the composer (www.michaelconwaybaker.com)

This quirky march was commissioned by and dedicated to Bob Rebagliati to celebrate his 25th year at Handsworthy Secondary School, North Vancouver, B.C. Mr. Baker is particularly fond of this march and feels it works exceptionally well for band. It also seems to be quite easy to put together. The quirky nature of the music comes from the fact that its genesis comes from a film cue the composer wrote characterizing a fish factory. One has only to imagine a huge factory mass-producing fish sticks to get a sense of the quirky nature of the place. (Michael Conway Baker)

A recording of this march is available from the composer.

The Mountains
Difficulty: Grade 3
Duration: 7:00
Composed in 1989
Available through CMC and the composer (www.michaelconwaybaker.com)

This music is the third movement of a suite called *Through the Lions' Gate*. Originally written for and performed by the Vancouver Symphony, this particular movement created a sensation when it was first performed. Since then there have been many performances throughout Canada and the U.S. Because of its popularity, Mr. Baker was commissioned by the Funabashi Festival in Japan to do a band arrangement for their festival. The music is very lyrical and characterizes the beauty of the mountains that surround Vancouver. There is a romantic piano part, which was recently simplified for less expert pianists. This work, in the words of the composer, is a "guaranteed crowd pleaser."

There is an orchestral recording on the Summit label as performed by the London Sinfonia. The title of the CD is "Hope's Journey," and all the music on the CD is by Mr. Baker. (Michael Conway Baker)

Okanagan Spring
Difficulty: Grade 3
Duration: 8:00
Composed in 1989
Available through CMC and the composer (www.michaelconwaybaker.com)

The Okanagan valley, in British Columbia, is one of the most colorful places on earth in the months of spring. This region is full of orchards which blossom during the months of April, May and June. The music attempts to capture the effect such beauty has on the viewer. Written for and dedicated to Wayne Jeffrey and his concert band at Kwantlen University, this music is, as the title implies, a light-hearted and, sometimes, impressionistic work. A clearly delineated tune in 5/8 time prevails throughout. (Michael Conway Baker)

ROBERT BAUER (B. 1950)

ROBERT PAUL BAUER BEGAN his musical studies at age seven. Throughout his youth he played guitar and saxophone in rock and dance bands, often arranging and composing for these ensembles. At the same time he was developing an interest in jazz and classical music and after high school he entered the Faculty of Music at the University of Toronto. There he studied Composition with John Beckwith and John Weinzweig, Materials of Music with Oskar Morawetz, Godfrey Ridout, Lothar Klein, Derek Holman and Gustav Ciamaga, saxophone with Paul Brodie and guitar with Eli Kassner. It was during these years that he began integrating some of the elements that are now a part of his personal style: rhythmic irregularity, angular melodic line with an underlying, often subtle, lyricism and a preoccupation with impressionistic tone colors.

Following his graduation in 1972 with a Bachelor of Music degree he became involved in the group ARRAYMUSIC and began teaching guitar at the Brodie School of Music. In 1976, he joined the CBC in Toronto, first as a technician and later as a producer. He also composed actively for his own instruments, both guitar and saxophone, as well as for mixed chamber ensembles through commissions from Paul Brodie, ARRAYMUSIC and others.

In 1980 his CBC work took him to Ottawa and the program "Mostly Music." There he was associated with conductor Peter McCoppin, and this led him to do some orchestral composition. He again composed much for the guitar—a duet for Wilson and McAllister, a Trio for the Amsterdam Guitar Trio and a solo work for Douglas Reach. One major work that bridges his Toronto/Ottawa years is Nocturne, which was commissioned by the CBC and premiered by New Music Concerts.

In 1988 Bauer relocated once again, this time to Halifax. Still with CBC Radio, he produced the network programs "Weekender" and "Music Alive." Currently he produces the extremely popular and quirky "Weekend Mornings" program for the Maritime region on CBC Radio One. The move to Halifax was a tremendous catalyst for Bauer's creativity. In 1990 he founded the new music and improvisational ensemble UPSTREAM. Bauer has written numerous works for this ensemble as well as its collaborations with Symphony Nova Scotia as part of the "Open Waters Festival of New and Improvised Music." He has been active as well in the Atlantic Canadian Composer's Association. In October of 2000 Bauer presented a retrospective concert of his chamber works titled *Spirit Through Time*. In March of 2002, he was one of three featured composers at the University of New Mexico's Composer's Symposium. (CMC)

Sanctus (for Symphonic Band)
Difficulty: Grade 4
Duration: 5:30
Composed in 2001
Available through CMC (www.musiccentre.ca)

Sanctus was commissioned by the Canadian Music Centre as part of its New Music for Young Musicians project. It was composed for the band of Charles P. Allen High School in Bedford, Nova Scotia, Nathan Beeler, conductor.

The New Music for Young Musicians project was an effort by the Canadian Music Centre to begin addressing the problem of a lack of contemporary music repertoire for young musicians. This was a millennium program for commissioning Canadian composers to write and distribute new compositions for young musicians to study and perform. The aim of the project was to address the need for engaging new repertoire for a wide variety of ensembles and instrumentations, and to make recent Canadian music more prominent in the musical lives of young performers. Initiated through the CMC and furthered by the partnerships of prominent educational organizations, more than 100 new pieces were commissioned across Canada. Thirty new works were commissioned through the CMC Ontario Region, as well as three new works contributed by composers in the Atlantic Region. With specific guidelines of duration, instrumentation, level of difficulty, and the knowledge that young players would perform the music, each composer approached the composition in his or her own unique way.

Sanctus provides improvisatory and vocal opportunities for the ensemble, with the tempo varying from quarter note = 76 to quarter note = 110. The work remains in the key of D minor throughout, and is primarily in 3/4 with an extended 7/4 section. The faster sections contain challenging woodwind passages but are playable by a school band.

The newly revised version of *Sanctus* (2006) has been subtitled: In memoriam Christine Webber. Christine Webber was a young music educator and French horn player who died prematurely and suddenly from complications due to asthma. She was one of the music teachers of the composer's son, and he appended this subtitle in admiration of her dedication. (CMC and interview with the composer)

ALLAN BELL (B. 1953)

CALGARY NATIVE ALLAN GORDON BELL received a Master of Music degree from the University of Alberta where he studied with Violet Archer, Malcolm Forsyth, and Manus Sasonkin. He also did advanced studies in composition at the Banff Centre for the Arts where his teachers were Jean Coulthard, Bruce Mather, and Oskar Morawetz.

He has created works for solo instruments, chamber ensembles, orchestra, band, and electroacoustic media. His works have been performed by many professional and amateur organizations in Canada, the United States, the United Kingdom, West Germany, Israel, and Japan. In 1988, his *Concerto for Two Orchestras* was performed at the Olympic Arts Festival; in 1989, his *Arche II* was performed by the finalists at the Banff International String Quartet Competition and was sent by the CBC as the English Network submission to the International Rostrum of Composers in Paris. In 1992, his *An Elemental Lyric* was performed at Carnegie Hall in New York, the Kennedy Centre in Washington, D.C., and Symphony Hall in Boston; and in 1996, his *Danse Sauvage* was the imposed piece for the 1996 Esther Honens International Piano Competition.

In further testament to his versatility, the Association of Canadian Choral Conductors presented him with an award for outstanding choral compositions in both 1994 and 1999. In February of 2001, the Calgary Opera Association and Quest Theatre presented the premiere performances of his chamber opera *Turtle Wakes*, and in August of 2001, Ensemble Resonance presented the Asian premiere of his *a great arch softening the mountains* at the Cantai International Festival in Taipei. In February of 2002, Bell was the distinguished visiting composer at the Winnipeg New Music Festival where the Winnipeg Symphony Orchestra performed four of his compositions. CBC Records has released a CD entitled "Spirit Trail: The Music of Allan Gordon Bell" that contains five of his orchestral pieces.

Bell is Professor of Music at the University of Calgary. From 1984 to 1988, he served as President of the National Board of the Canadian Music Centre. (CMC, The Canadian Encyclopedia, and www.composers21.com)

From Chaos to the Birth of a Dancing Star
Difficulty: Grade 4
Duration: 8:00
Composed in 1983
Available through CMC (www.musiccentre.ca)

Dissonant tone clusters, aleatoric notation, sprung rhythm, minimalist ostinati, changing meters, and unusual sound effects are explored in Allan Bell's programmatic *From Chaos to the Birth of a Dancing Star*. Bell composed the work on a commission from the Alberta Band Association while he was working with students at a high school in Edmonton.

The composer writes, *"From Chaos to the Birth of a Dancing Star* was created in response to the week that I spent as a 'composer in the school' working with the students at Salisbury Composite High School on the notions surrounding creativity in music. During the course of our explorations the students created an evocative piece that they called *From Chaos to Tranquility.* The piece had many strengths and intriguing musical gestures. As well, the title reminded me of an epigram from the philosopher, Friedrich Nietzsche. In describing the creative process, he wrote that it is only through chaos that there can be the birth of a dancing star. Hence, from Nietzsche and the students comes the title of this piece. The work follows the program of the title, from the violence of the opening, through the introduction of a short melodic motif and its development as a melody with orchestrational variations, to its serene conclusion." (CMC and Patricia Shand)

A pedagogical discussion of this work can be found on page 41 of *Guidelist of Unpublished Canadian Band Music Suitable for Student Performers* by Patricia Martin Shand.

A recording of this work is available on the CD, "Reflections on the Past," Arktos 99033CD, by the University of Calgary Wind Ensemble.

In the Eye of the Four Winds
Difficulty: Grade 3
Duration: 13:00
Composed in 1986
Available through CMC (www.musiccentre.ca)

In the Eye of the Four Winds was created to celebrate the centennial of Lethbridge Public School District #51. It had its premiere on October 24, 1986 at the Glenbow Theatre in Calgary, with the composer conducting the University of Calgary Wind Ensemble, and is dedicated to the memory of the composer's father.

The composer writes: At the center of a raging wind lies a still point, the so-called "eye of the storm." Traditionally, humanity has had strong convictions about the character of the winds that blow from the four cardinal points of the compass. This piece is an attempt to capture both the power of the wind and the spirit that lies at the center of each of the four directions, the spirit that lies in the eye of four winds.

The piece contains several fingerprints of Bell's style, such as an abundance of rhythmic syncopation and jazz-influenced figures, as well as prominent material presented by the percussion section.

Structurally the piece consists of nine short movements—a vigorous prelude, three interludes and a postlude that are variations upon the prelude, and the four winds. Each of the winds features a soloist and a sound created by the flow of air through the mouths of the members of the ensemble. The soloists for each of the four "winds" can be chosen from among the following options:

North: trumpet or horn
South: trombone, baritone or tuba
East: flute or clarinet
West: alto or tenor saxophone, or bass clarinet

(CMC and The Canadian Encyclopedia)

KENNETH BRAY (1919–1999)

A GRADUATE OF THE University of Toronto (Bachelor of Music) and the Eastman School of Music, University of Rochester (Master of Music), Kenneth Bray began piano lessons at age five, and later studied tuba in high school and bassoon at university level. Before war service in World War II with the Royal Canadian Air Force, he was a music supervisor in several Muskoka District (Ontario) schools. After university studies, he taught high school, later serving on faculties at the universities of Toronto and Western Ontario. He was active in teaching, performing, arranging and composing music most of his life. He has many choral and instrumental publications to his credit and co-authored the following series: For Young Musicians, Solos for Schools, and Reflections of Canada. He was president of the Ontario Music Educators Association, the Canadian Music Educators Association, and the Kodály Institute of Canada. He also was a founding member of the London Festival Brass and the London Woodwind Quintet, and played bassoon with the London Symphony Orchestra.

Bray taught summer courses and served on music curriculum review committees for the Ontario Ministry of Education prior to his appointment in 1969 to the Faculty of Music, University of Western Ontario. There he taught theory, orchestration, aural training, and bassoon until his retirement as professor emeritus in 1984. (Orchestra London Canada, The Canadian Encyclopedia, and Eighth Note Publications, used by permission)

Reverie for Bonita
Difficulty: Grade 3
Duration: 2:30
Published 1998 by Eighth Note Publications (www.enpmusic.com)

A lush and beautiful work composed by Kenneth Bray for his daughter, *Reverie for Bonita* features the horn section, full use of mutes and simple, elegant themes. Showing off the lyrical side of the band, this work is an ideal "mood change" during a concert. (© Eighth Note Publications, used by permission)

Bob Buckley (B. 1946)

Bob Buckley has been active as a composer, arranger, performer, producer, and conductor in Canada and around the world for more than 30 years. The diverse nature of his background has given him the opportunity to write for almost every genre. He was born in Brighton, England, and now divides his time between England and Vancouver, BC, Canada.

He took up the piano at the age of ten and began composing soon thereafter. He began his formal music studies with California composer Hubert Klyne Headley, who exposed him to the twentieth century music of Stravinsky, Bartok, Ravel, and Shostakovitch. He then went on to study composition, conducting and arranging with American composer William Bergsma at the University of Washington, and electronic music at the University of British Columbia.

Upon leaving university Buckley started working professionally and appeared regularly on television. In his quest to combine rock, jazz and symphonic music he formed the band "Spring," with which he had his first top ten single, and performed the original work *Song Cycle* with the Vancouver and Edmonton Symphonies. Then, recording on CBS Records and A&M Records, he contributed to five albums containing several top-ten singles and a gold record with the number one single *Letting Go.*

During this time he worked professionally as a composer, arranger, performer, producer and conductor for records, theme music for television series and specials, commercials, audio-visuals, dances, musicals, symphonic works and films. In 1986 he composed *This Is My Home* for the Canada Pavilion at Expo '86, a song that has been performed at every Canada Day since and has become like a second National Anthem. He also composed the music for the opening and closing ceremonies of the 1994 Commonwealth Games in Victoria, B.C. He did string arrangements for albums by Bryan Adams, Celine Dion, Aerosmith, Motley Crue, Our Lady Peace; and composed two musicals for the Charlottetown Festival, one of which has been running for nine years. Buckley has scored hundreds of television programs including the award winning computer-animated series "Reboot," "Transformers," and "Shadow Raiders," and most recently the computer-animated movies "Casper's Haunted Christmas" and "Scary Godmother." (Interview with the composer)

The Cascadia Suite: *Cascadia, Cathedral Grove,* **and** *Sea to Sky*
Difficulty: Grade 3
Duration: 9:19
Published 2007 by Fentone Publishing (www.fentone.com)

The Cascadia Suite is a three-movement work originally commissioned in 1996 to celebrate the tenth anniversary of the Summer Pops Youth Orchestra of Vancouver, Garth Williams and Jim Littleford, Music Directors. Each movement is a musical depiction of one of the natural scenic wonders of British Columbia, and contains themes written for the 1994 Commonwealth Games held in Victoria, BC. The composer has rescored each of these reflections of the mountains, lakes, and rivers of the west for concert band. Although designed to be played in sequence, each movement may be performed separately.

1. Cascadia (2:55) is a tone poem saluting the grandeur of the Cascades and the lands that lie below them. It opens at a brisk tempo (quarter note = 120 throughout) with a declamatory statement in the horns and saxophones that clearly is designed to evoke a mountain scene. Bold and forward moving, it is marked by triplet figures for all players in the final section.

2. Cathedral Grove (3:36) takes the listener into the stillness of the arboreal forest with the ferns and salal underfoot and the overarching majesty of the giants of the forest. The horn has an opening solo against an andante cantabile background in 12/8 meter, with crescendos and diminuendos creating the feeling of swaying trees. Brass and woodwinds take turns with two-measure phrases, and a brief rallentando and decrescendo bring the movement to a quiet close.

3. Sea to Sky (2:48) celebrates the Sea to Sky Highway that winds its way past scenic Howe Sound and the snow clad Tantalus mountain range to the Whistler Ski Resort, site of the 2010 Winter Olympics. The piece begins gently, reflecting the ocean scenery, and builds to a fanfare as the glaciers and peaks come into view. A cantabile follows, bringing the listener back down to the tranquility of the scenery. The main theme returns and is developed as Whistler Mountain itself comes into view. (© De Haske Publications BV, used by permission)

Millennium March
Difficulty: Grade 3
Duration: 3:16
Published 2000 by NS Musico Publishing (www.nsmusico.com)

As the title implies, this march was written to celebrate the new millennium. It was first performed by the Douglas College Band in New Westminster, BC and the North Shore Concert Band in North Vancouver, Canada. The clarinets and flutes will find challenging parts in the fast paced composition. Favorable key signatures (B-flat and E-flat) make lighter work of it all, and reflect the composer's working knowledge of these instruments. Written in standard march form, the work begins in 6/8, moves to 2/4 at the trio, and remains in 2/4 to the finale. (© NS Musico Publishing, used by permission)

Pacifica
Difficulty: Grade 4
Duration: 5:05
Published 2001 by NS Musico Publishing (www.nsmusico.com)

This composition was the winner of the Canadian Composer's Award from the Ontario chapter of the Canadian Band Association in 1993. It was written to celebrate the beauty of the Pacific Northwest region of the United States and Canada.

The opening theme's energetic air (allegro ritmico, quarter note = 132) brings to mind the busy, bustling coastal ports and cities. A sensitive clarinet solo slows the pace down (quarter note = 82) to the stillness of a quiet lagoon or lake. The piece returns to the original theme, and finishes at a driving allegro tempo with a soaring orchestral theme echoing the drama and majesty of the mountainous coastal fjords and the Rockies. (© NS Musico Publishing, used by permission)

Shadow Play
Difficulty: Grade 4
Duration: 7:20
Published 2004 by NS Musico Publishing (www.nsmusico.com)

Shadow Play was written for the North Shore Concert Band in Vancouver, BC, Canada, and was premiered by the Band of the Fifteenth Field Regiment, Royal Canadian Artillery, Captain Richard Van Slyke, conducting. The work strives to represent the interplay between matter and energy, time and space, light and dark. There are excellent solos for soprano saxophone (cued for clarinet) and flugelhorn, and the subtle interplay between instruments makes this an excellent work to teach the concept of call and response. The work achieves a thoughtful and pensive mood throughout, with easily executed meter changes and dynamic contrasts. Soprano saxophone and flugelhorn are again featured as the work achieves a soft and restful conclusion. (© NS Musico Publishing, used by permission)

Theme from "ReBoot"
Difficulty: Grade 4
Duration: 3:35
Published 2003 by NS Musico Publishing (www.nsmusico.com)

"ReBoot" was the first television series produced entirely with computer graphics, and Buckley wrote the theme, songs, and series score. Created in Vancouver, BC, it premiered in the U.S. in 1994 and has been shown in 70 countries around the world. The action takes place in Mainframe, a computer on the internet, and the episodes center around the hero Matrix and the evil Megabyte and the equally brutal Hexadecimal. Good always conquers evil in the final moments of each episode. "ReBoot" was the number one children's show in North America, Europe, and Asia for several years. The theme was first performed by the North Shore Concert Band in Vancouver, and a recording is available through their website, www.northshorebands.com.

Written almost entirely in 5/4, this piece would be an excellent way to introduce students to Gustav Holst's *Mars* without that work's feeling of doom and destruction. The piece begins with a heroic theme to portray Matrix, drops into a dark passage to signify the villains, then returns to the original theme in a triumphant flourish. (© NS Musico Publishing, used by permission)

This is My Home *for band and choir*
Difficulty: Grade 3
Duration: 3:47
Published 1986 by NS Musico Publishing (www.nsmusico.com)

In 1986 twenty two million people visited Expo '86 in Vancouver, BC. The centerpiece of the fair was the Canadian Pavilion, and when people first entered the building they were brought into a large multi-media theatre where they were treated to the presentation "This Is My Home." Images of Canada-the land, its icons and its people-flashed around the room and the strains of *This is my Home* soared over it all. It has become an unofficial second anthem of sorts, and is played annually on Parliament Hill in Ottawa on Canada Day with full symphony and a massive choir.

This concert band arrangement is true to the symphonic original, and with singers and choir it is a stirring work guaranteed to be a climax to any Canadian assembly. A choir with male and female soloists is required. The optional children's choir parts can be performed by the main choir. (© NS Musico Publishing, used by permission)

Thunderbird March
Difficulty: Grade 3
Duration: 2:47
Published 2004 by NS Musico Publishing (www.nsmusico.com)

This march was written in 1987 to commemorate the 50th anniversary of the founding of the North Vancouver Youth Band. It premiered at the reunion concert, held at the Orpheum Theater that same year. An alumni band was recruited from former members, who shared the stage that evening with the youth band. Many of these players were drawn from the then fledgling North Vancouver Alumni Band, which grew to become the North Shore Concert Band.

Thunderbird March begins in 2/4 time in F major and follows standard march format, changing key to B-flat major at the trio. To add interest to the piece, however, the composer also changes the meter to 6/8 just before reaching the trio. The final strain is played at a full forte to bring the march to a satisfying close. This contemporary march features moderate ranges and interesting parts for all sections. (© NS Musico Publishing, used by permission)

WALTER BUCZYNSKI (B. 1933)

WALTER BUCZYNSKI STUDIED PIANO with Earle Moss and composition with Godfrey Ridout. He won second prizes in CAPAC (Composers, Authors and Publishers Association of Canada) competitions in 1951 and 1952 with a piano sonata and songs, and a first prize in 1954 with a piano trio. He studied in 1955 at Aspen with Darius Milhaud and Charles Jones, and won a Fromm Foundation Award with the *Suite for Woodwind Quintet.* Later teachers included Rosina Lhévinne and Zbigniew Drzewiecki for piano, and, for composition, Nadia Boulanger. From 1962–69 he taught piano and theory at the Royal Conservatory of Music in Toronto. He began teaching these subjects and composition at the University of Toronto in 1969. As a solo pianist he debuted in 1955 with the Toronto Symphony Orchestra in Chopin's *F Minor Concerto.* During the 1960's and early 1970's he made solo recordings and gave solo concerts in New York, Paris, Warsaw, and many Canadian cities, as well as CBC radio recitals, featuring his own and other contemporary Canadian works in addition to standard repertoire. He was president 1974–5 of the Canadian League of Composers, and in 1976 received the Queen Elizabeth medal for his contribution to the Polish musical scene in Canada.

For many years, Buczynski's dual commitment to the piano and composition found him giving one, then the other, his attention. In 1977, however, he decided to curtail his pianistic career in view of the increased demands of teaching and composing, and gave few concerts afterwards—exceptions being his all-Buczynski program in Toronto in 1982, and recitals after 1990. Antonín Kubálek gave a recital of Buczynski's piano music in 1979, later broadcast by the CBC, and the CBC and the University of Toronto Faculty of Music co-sponsored a 50th birthday concert of his works in December 1983.

An exceptionally prolific composer, Buczynski has been repeatedly commissioned by prominent Canadian artists such as Kubálek (*Piano Concerto, Piano Sonata No. 3*), William Aide (*Suite One-Two-Three, Lyric 1*), Joseph Macerollo (*'Kind of Popular' Pieces, Divertissement No. 2, Litanies*), and the Purcell String Quartet (*Quartet No. 3, Quartet No. 4, Piano Quintet*), and organizations such as NMC, ARRAYMUSIC, the Montreal International Music Competition, and the CBC.

Buczynski retired from the University of Toronto in 1999. His 70th birthday was celebrated extensively in the Toronto music community with several concerts and performances. (CMC, The Canadian Encyclopedia, The Canadian Music Encyclopedia, and interview with the composer)

The Trilogy of the 2238 *(Taking the 2238, Dreaming on the 2238, Arriving on the 2238)*
Difficulty: Grade 5
Duration: 19:40
Composed 1993–1995
Available through CMC (www.musiccentre.ca)

The Trilogy of the 2238 was the composer's first work for band. It was commissioned by Cameron Walter, a former pupil of the composer, for the University of Toronto Wind Symphony, and premiered by that group. The composer says, "Somehow, nearly everyone is sure that the 2238 is a locomotive; if so, I did take advantage of that impression. The work is more of an inward glance, and refers to pages two to thirty-eight in the score [of the first movement]. After hearing the first movement of the piece, many people got the impression that this was a train, so I decided to continue in this medium. I hope [everyone appreciates] the humor of it all."

Each movement may be performed separately, and the openings of all three are connected/similar. Movement one, *Taking the 2238* (6:38), written in 1993, is somewhat aggressive and does indeed give the impression of a train. Movement two, *Dreaming on the 2238* (6:30), was composed in 1994 and continues the train motif; the listener may imagine him/herself in a dream state in a Pullman car as the train speeds through the night. Movement three, *Arriving on the 2238* (6:00), was written in 1995, and brings the traveler "home" by reintroducing the opening motives of movement one. (Interview with the composer)

A recording of the second movement of this work is available on the CD "Dreaming on the 2238" by the University of Toronto Wind Symphony, and may be obtained through the Canadian Music Centre.

LLOYD BURRITT (B. 1940)

WHEN LLOYD BURRITT WAS in his teens he took piano lessons from Ira Swartz, Elaine Korman, and Annette Atlee. He studied at the University of British Columbia with Jean Coulthard (composition) and Donald Brown and Marie Schilder (voice), and in England at the Royal College of Music 1963–5 with Herbert Howells and Gordon Jacob (composition). At Tanglewood (summers 1965, 1966) he studied conducting with Leonard Bernstein, Erich Leinsdorf, Dee Hiatt, and Gunther Schuller. Returning to the University of British Columbia, he worked 1966–8 in electronic music under Courtland Hultberg.

In 1964 Burritt began teaching in schools in the Vancouver area, and from 1970 he taught at Argyle Secondary School, first music and, from 1981–99, theater and composition. In the late 1970's he served on the music curriculum committee for British Columbia, for which he designed composition courses. Burritt has composed on commission for the Vancouver Symphony Orchestra (*Assassinations, Fanfare,* and *Electric Tongue*); the CBC (*Spectrum* and incidental music for *Peer Gynt*); the National Arts Centre Orchestra (*Overdose*); the RCCO (*Memo to RCCO*); Hugh McLean (*Icon*); the Canadian Music Centre; and the Vancouver Lesbian and Gay Choir. In 1986 he was commissioned to write *Song for Marshall McLuhan* for the opening ceremony in the Canada Pavilion at Expo '86. His works often employ texts and reveal literary associations and influences; they also display a profound spiritual sense, especially in *Altar of the Sun* (1983), which was written as a result of a trip to Italy and inspired by the life and teachings of St Francis of Assisi. His works have been performed by major ensembles in Canada, the USA, Great Britain, and Sweden. Burritt uses sounds coloristically and employs repeated patterns to produce a freely structured expressionist music. (CMC and interview with composer)

Crystal Earth (1987–1992)
Difficulty: Grade 4
Duration: 9:45
Composed in 1987
Available through CMC (www.musiccentre.ca)

The titles of this four-movement work are inspired by the "Save Our Planet Ecology Movement" during the 1980's. These titles clearly define the mood of each movement: *I - Awakening; II - Window of Light; III - Stepping Stones; and IV - Crystal Earth.* Movements I and II (3:00 each), III (3:30), and IV (3:15) may be performed independently.

Awakening is an allegro sixteen bar fanfare for full band that leads directly to the slow and quiet *Window of Light.* Upper woodwinds begin this lovely contrapuntal movement and are joined by the full ensemble at its climax. The movement closes with quiet brass. *Stepping Stones,* a march in cut time, opens with an alto saxophone solo in a rhythmic scherzo. Clarinets pick up the motif and pass it to the flutes and clarinets. Tutti trumpets invert the motif, and then move to an espressivo section with flutes, clarinets and trumpets playing the motif. Tutti chords bridge the development of the motif while the meter alternates between cut time and 3/4. *Crystal Earth,* in a cantabile 3/4, is built on an eighth note ostinato figure to suggest the turning of planet earth in its orbit around the sun. The ostinato opens in the upper woodwinds against lower woodwinds and brass sustained chords. Sixteenths and a triplet eighth figure are introduced and carry through the final measures to imply that our planet never stops turning.

Movement IV - *Crystal Earth's* text was inspired by the Quetzalcoatl Prophecies and the Mayan calendar system, which reflects the agricultural, political and ritual needs characteristic of Mayan society. The director may wish to substitute flute solo in place of the soprano solo and echo brass quartet in place of the mixed chorus. The composer recommends printing the text in the concert program. (CMC and interview with the composer)

Gabriola Gambol for Symphonic Winds
Difficulty: Grade 5
Duration: 5:00
Available through CMC (www.musiccentre.ca)

This work premiered in April 2006, and subsequently was performed twice in Ireland the following month. The inspiration for this piece is Gabriola Island, which sits off shore from the city of Nanaimo on Vancouver Island, B.C. Gabriola Island is on the western edge of Georgia Straight, and dolphins are frequently sighted from the island. "Gambol" means to dance and skip in play or frolic. *Gabriola Gambol* begs the question, "What is life anyway...but to gambol like dolphins...to dance and skip in play...to frolic in Coastal waters." Sighting dolphins brings us good luck and sends our spirit soaring.

In the opening andante 9/8 of this introspective, atmospheric seascape, Burritt introduces an eighth note theme in the piano, and shimmering eighths in the marimba are set against sustained upper woodwinds. The theme transfers to the piccolo, then the clarinet, while the counterpoint moves to the bassoon. The return of the andante 9/8 repeats solos in the oboe and piccolo, bridging to a waltz that showcases a sumptuous English horn solo. Counterpoint in the French horn builds and accelerates into an allegro finale, where full percussion drives the gambol to its joyfully climactic ending.

"I've been told dolphins like to gambol in these waters and sighting them brings good luck." (Barbara Kingsolver, "Where the Map Stopped," New York Times, 1992) (Interview with the composer)

Passage Island
Difficulty: Grade 5
Duration: 5:00
Composed in 2001
Available through CMC (www.musiccentre.ca)

Passage Island was commissioned by the West Vancouver Youth Band, Douglas Macaulay, Director, in 2001 and premiered in the same year. The material was derived from the composer's *Overture* for orchestra (1980), which was commissioned, premiered and recorded by the New Caledonia Orchestra in Prince George.

The inspiration for this piece is Passage Island itself, which sits in the mouth of Howe Sound on the eastern edge of Georgia Straight. It is located twenty minutes west of the city of Vancouver, B.C. The island is a tiny rock in size. While only a handful of homes dot its shoreline, hundreds and hundreds of boats of all sizes and description float on past this tiny island. Kayaks, sailboats, motor boats, tug boats pulling barges and log booms, freighters and ocean liners on their way to the Orient wash Passage Island's shore line with their wake.

Burritt's majestic maestoso 4/4 opening suggests the passing of a magnificent ocean liner. As it disappears over the horizon the music shifts into a con moto section that conjures Oriental imagery with solos in the oboe, soprano saxophone, flute, English horn, and bassoon. The orchestra bells wash over the island's shore, with accented repetition in the woodwinds and weaving brass canonic themes. The image is one of many boats of different sizes and description moving by in both directions. The work ends in tutti fortissimo chords. (CMC and interview with the composer)

HOWARD CABLE (B. 1920)

AN ICON AMONG CANADIAN artists, Howard Cable has been called the most successful conductor, composer, and arranger in Canadian music since the 1940s. He has been a leading figure in the musical life of Canada for over 60 years, and has done much to bring a sense of professionalism and virtuosity to band music and its performance in Canada. He studied at the Royal Conservatory of Music in Toronto with Sir Ernest MacMillan, Ettore Mazzoleni and Healey Willan. His early years were spent in radio when he succeeded Percy Faith on CBC in 1941. He has composed and conducted over 1000 radio dramas and variety programs. For several years, the Howard Cable Concert Band was heard nationally on the CBC and throughout the U.S. on the Mutual Radio Network. On television, he was musical director and arranger for many celebrated telecasts, including the highly popular "Showtime."

Cable's familiarity with a broad range of repertoire has kept him in demand as a composer and arranger for the Elmer Iseler Singers, the Toronto Mendelssohn Choir, the Toronto Children's Chorus, True North Brass and the Hannaford Street Silver Band. This has resulted in the recording of his compositions and arrangements on many record labels and performances of them worldwide.

His work in musical theater has led to notable collaborations. On Broadway, he arranged for Richard Rodgers, Meredith Willson and Frank Loesser. In the entertainment world, he has conducted for Ella Fitzgerald, Tony Bennett, Peggy Lee, Bob Hope, Victor Borge and Danny Kaye. In Canada, his theatrical credits include appearances as guest conductor at the Banff and Shaw festivals, and he has provided numerous scores for the Charlottetown Festival.

His 20-year association with the Canadian Brass resulted in his writing over 80 compositions and arrangements. He has arranged for the Canadian Brass collaboration with the Mormon Tabernacle Choir as well as their Lincoln Center concerts with the New York Philharmonic Brass.

He is a Member of the Order of Canada, one of Canada's highest civilian honors, in recognition of his lifetime of distinguished service to Canadian music. (CMC, Northdale Music Press, The Canadian Encyclopedia, Order of Canada, Timothy Maloney, and interview with the composer)

The Banks of Newfoundland
Difficulty: Grade 4
Duration: 7:30
Published 2007 by Eighth Note Publications (www.enpmusic.com)

This new edition of Howard Cable's *Newfoundland Rhapsody* with a full score is a long-awaited addition to the band library. Five years after Columbus discovered America, the explorer John Cabot claimed Newfoundland for England. It became Canada's tenth province in 1948. On the island, singing and song making have always been a part of everyday life. The material in this work is a sampling of popular sea songs and ballads, traditional and composed.

Cable skillfully joins eight Newfoundland folk songs in this work. *We'll Rant and We'll Roar Like True Newfoundlanders* is the island's theme tune. The words were written in 1880 and set to an English air. *The Sailing Cruise of the Lone Flier* is considered to be one of the finest airs in the Dorian mode. Variants have been found in several places in the United States. *Petty Harbour Bait Skiff* marks a tragedy at sea. It is a composed folk song by a national bard, John Grace, written in the late 19th century. (Also see the note for this song as arranged by Jim Duff.) *The Badger Drive*, composed by the bard John Devine, celebrates the winter months, when fishermen leave their nets to work in logging camps in the interior. *The Wreck of the Hemmer Jane* is known by more titles and carries more verses than most folksongs. In the United States it is the famous 49ers song *Sweet Betsy from Pike*. *Up the Pond* is known as the tune played for the August regatta day in St. John's, the capital. This event began in the mid 19th century. In march tempo, it is the regimental march of the Royal Newfoundland Regiment. *I'se the B'y* is the most popular square dance, foot-stompin' song on the island. Mr. Cable finishes the work in exciting style with *The Kelligrew's Soiree*, a much-loved "land" song written by the bard Johnny Burke around 1910. See also the note on *Newfoundland Rhapsody* below. (Interview with the composer and Eighth Note Publications, used by permission)

Berczy Portraits
Difficulty: Grade 3
Duration: 10:00
Published 2007 by Eighth Note Publications (www.enpmusic.com)

This is Howard Cable's homage to William Berczy, considered to be Canada's most important pre-Confederation artist. He made his mark in Canadian history as co-founder of Toronto, founder of Markham, Ontario and as an architect and celebrated portrait painter. He brought to pre-confederation Canada the influences of the 18th century art movement in Europe.

The first portrait is of the Woolsey family of Montreal, painted in 1809, the only group portrait in an interior setting to be found in pre-confederation art. The second is of William Berczy's wife Charlotte, painted in 1791. The third depicts the portrait of the war chief of the Mohawks, Joseph Brant, completed in 1807. Berczy had a close association with the Mohawk Confederacy and Chief Brant in establishing the Berczy settlers in Upper Canada. Brantford Ontario is named after Joseph Brant. (© Eighth Note Publications, used by permission)

Fiat Lux
Difficulty: Grade 4
Duration: 3:30
Published 2007 by Eighth Note Publications (www.enpmusic.com)

Fiat Lux means "Let there be light," and is the motto of the University of Lethbridge, Alberta. In 1951, during the war in Korea, Canada's National Defense Department produced a radio series on The CBC titled "Voice of the Army." The Howard Cable Concert Band was the mainstay of this patriotic/public relations program. Half the musical content was military, the balance 50's pop. Thirty-nine programs were produced, and each program required two marches. Mr. Cable composed eight marches for "Voice of the Army," and at the war's end the music went to storage. Some years later he reconstructed several of these forgotten scores, one of which is *Fiat Lux*, which he has dedicated to the University of Lethbridge. (© Eighth Note Publications, used by permission)

A recording of this work is available on the CD "McIntyre Ranch Country – Songs of the West," by the Lethbridge Community Gold Band, and may be ordered from their website, www.lcbs.ca/index.html.

Good Medicine – A Charlie Russell Suite
Difficulty: Grade 4
Duration: 16:00
Published 2007 by Eighth Note Publications (www.enpmusic.com)

Good Medicine is the second of two commissions by Mr. Ralph A. Thrall Jr., and was premiered by the Lethbridge Community Gold Band of Lethbridge, Alberta on October 22, 2005. Charles Marion Russell (1864–1926) was many things: consummate Westerner, historian, advocate of the Northern Plains Indians, cowboy, outdoorsman, writer, philosopher, environmentalist and conservationist, and not least, artist of the Old West. He worked as a cowboy and wrangler for more than a decade, all the while sketching and documenting the activities and excitement of the cow camp. He married in 1896, and painted and sculpted in his log studio adjacent to their home, filling it with his collection of Indian clothing, utilitarian objects, cowboy gear, horse jewelry, and other western props useful in accurately depicting the scenes of the Old West of which he was so fond. Charlie Russell completed approximately 4,000 works of art, and was the first "Western" artist to live the majority of his life in the West. *Good Medicine* is a work in four movements based on four of his paintings; *A Bronc to Breakfast, The Tie Rope, Waiting for a Chinook,* and *Ask the Horse*. Highly descriptive and reflective of the paintings that inspired them, each movement is accessible and contains interesting percussion parts. Solos by trumpet and euphonium are easily executed. Key signatures are primarily in F, Bb, and Eb, and the last 40 measures are in Db. (Notes from the premiere concert program and interview with the composer)

Hard Oil
Difficulty: Grade 4
Duration: 11:00
Published 2007 by Eighth Note Publications (www.enpmusic.com)

The history of the oil industry that spans the world began in 1855 in Oil Springs, Lambton Country, Ontario. This discovery was one year before the discovery in Pennsylvania. Today the mystery is gone and the thrill of discovery is no more, but the goal of this highly descriptive musical work is to make certain that history does not forget that, for a time, Canada led the world in terms of the petroleum industry. *Hard Oil* is a reminiscence of that first quest for oil in the last half of the 19th century.

The composer describes the movements:

1. The Drillers
By the 1870's Lambton Country Oil drillers were world famous and were in all major oil fields in the world. When the hard oilers (as they were called) left for far-off fields, the town band would play *Will Ye No Come Back Again* as the train pulled out.

2. The Jerker Lines
John Henry Fairbank, founder of Fairbank Oil (which is still in operation) devised a system of hooking up multiple wells with ground-level long wooden poles powered by one steam engine. Fairbank put the system, called "jerker lines," into his fields in 1865, and this mid-19th century technology is still working today—24/7.

3. The Gusher
The very first gusher blew in Oil Springs in 1862. Hugh Nixon Show, known as "that insane Yankee," had almost given up when a loud boom was heard over the countryside and the world's largest gusher spread oil up to a foot thick, and flowed freely for weeks before it was choked off. Oil Springs, Ontario is still known as the home of the first commercial oil well, and several producers are still extracting oil from the original fields.

(Interview with the composer and Eighth Note Publications, used by permission)

Marchmanship
Difficulty: Grade 3
Duration: 2:45
Published 1959 by Chappell (out of print)

This is one of Cable's first marches, written for Chappell Music at their request shortly after he began to write for that company. He had achieved a reputation in the U.S. as an excellent composer and arranger, primarily through CBC radio broadcasts of his concert band in the early 1950's. The superb scoring, dynamic contrasts, and syncopation of this march cause it to stand out from other marches of that same era. (Band Music Notes and interview with the composer)

McIntyre Ranch Country
Difficulty: Grade 4
Duration: 11:15
Published 2007 by Eighth Note Publications (www.enpmusic.com)

McIntyre Ranch Country was composed at the request of Ralph A. Thrall Jr., owner of the McIntyre Ranch in McGrath, Alberta, and is a collage of some of

Mr. Thrall's favorite western songs. The piece commemorates the history and beauty of the 55,000 acre McIntyre Ranch, located south of Lethbridge, Alberta. The ranch is world renowned for its ranching practices, scenic vastness and commitment to the preservation of the natural grasslands, habitat and wildlife. *McIntyre Ranch Country* received its premiere at the concert "Cable's Country'" performed with the Lethbridge Community Gold Band and the Lethbridge University Singers on October 5, 2002.

The work begins with *Cowboy's Gettin-Up Holler* and moves directly into *The Old Chisholm Trail. I Ride an Old Paint* and *Git Along Little Dogies* follow, with tempo and meter changes that allow for much expression. *The Streets of Laredo* comes next in a slow 3/4 that changes to a "galloping one-in-a-bar" tempo to accommodate *The Railroad Corral.* A molto rallentando leads to *Good-by Old Paint* and the highly evocative Blackfoot *Owl Dance.* Many of these cowboy songs would serve as excellent teaching examples of pentatonic melody. This well-written work would be an excellent addition to a concert with a Western or cowboy theme. (Interview with the composer and Eighth Note Publications, used by permission)

A recording of this work is available on the CD "McIntyre Ranch Country – Songs of the West," by the Lethbridge Community Gold Band, and may be ordered from their website, www.lcbs.ca/index.html.

Newfoundland Rhapsody
Difficulty: Grade 5
Duration: 7:50
Published 1956 by Chappell (out of print)

During the 1950's and 60s, Howard Cable composed a group of band works on Canadian folk tunes that were published by Chappell and won him recognition throughout North America. Probably the best known of these works is *Newfoundland Rhapsody,* which dates from 1956. The piece is a lilting and nautical collection of Newfoundland folk songs that range from the boisterous, to the humorous, to the poignant, to the completely outrageous. It also is not easy to perform, having been written for his professional band that performed weekly on CBC radio.

The composition achieves much of its variety through continuous manipulation of ritards, accelerandi, and pauses. Meters include 3/8, 3/4, and 6/8. Given appropriate direction by an experienced conductor, the players' greatest challenges are in solo parts. The trombone part in particular requires a confident player with a strong upper range. Cable's choice of keys can also be daunting for inexperienced players (for example, the climactic passage in *Up the Pond,* which has the low brass in C-flat Major), but the piece constitutes some of the most satisfying music ever written for wind band. The folk tunes include *We'll Rant and We'll Roar Like True Newfoundlanders, The Sealing Cruise of the Lone Flier, The Petty Harbor Bait Skiff, The Wreck of the Emma Jane* (which sounds very much like *Sweet Betsy from Pike),* and *Up the Pond.* This brilliantly scored work is out of print but may still be found in larger, well-established libraries. See also the note on *The Banks of Newfoundland* above. (CMC, Keith Kinder, and Michael Purves-Smith)

A recording of this work is available on the CD "Concert in the Park," disk number SMCD5079, by the Edmonton Wind Ensemble, and may be ordered from the Canadian Music Centre (www.musiccentre.ca).

O Canada
Difficulty: Grade 4
Duration: 1:15
Published 1996 by Northdale Music Press (www.northdalemusic.com)

O Canada, Canada's national anthem, was written by Calixa Lavallée (1842–1891) for the French Canadian National Festival held in Québec City during the Saint Jean Baptiste festivities, June 23–25, 1880. The original lyrics, in French, were the contribution of Adolphe-Basile Routhier. Beginning in 1901, English lyrics written by various lyricists were heard across the country. One hundred years after its first performance, *O Canada* was officially proclaimed national anthem of Canada, with French lyrics by Routhier and English lyrics by Robert Stanley Weir. Modifications to the English lyrics were made in 1968. The French lyrics remain unchanged.

Howard Cable's notes on *O Canada:*

"My first published arrangement of *O Canada* was written for Expo '67 and, as the official anthem, was played throughout that Montreal summer. Musicians enjoyed the startling tonality change (F to A flat) but sing-along audiences hated the arrangement because the key was too high and the key change made them very irritable. Ironically, the publisher was an American conglomerate that jettisoned the entire catalogue in the 1970's and ceased operation, thus making a collector's item out of *Modular Lavallée*. This arrangement is of a more agreeable nature—a singable key, fully scored with no key changes. In addition, it contains a small tribute to one of the most significant creators of our time." In paying this compliment, Cable is referring to Benjamin Britten.

(Keith Kinder, A Young Person's Guide to the Orchestra, and Northdale Music Press, used by permission)

Ontario Pictures
Difficulty: Grade 5
Duration: 8:15 (3:13 + 2:30 + 2:30)
Published 1993 by Northdale Music Press (www.northdalemusic.com)

Ontario Pictures is one of six pieces for concert band that premièred July 1, 1986 at the Canada and Ontario Pavilions at Expo 86 in Vancouver. Funded by the Ontario Arts Council, the Northdale Concert Band commissioned six composers to create six-minute works to mark the International Year of Canadian Music.

Each composer was requested to create an entertaining piece appropriate for national and heritage events—to provide melodic, festive, and accessible music to foster the atmosphere of a celebration. Cable's composition was the first of these six works to be published. It is a work in three movements for senior high school, post-secondary, community, or professional concert band.

Toronto Star music critic William Littler referred to the piece as "brightly-painted sketches evoking the atmosphere of Thunder Bay, Point Pelee and the 19th century world of Kingston's Fort Henry"— a reference to the name of each of the three movements. *Ontario Pictures* is a melodically pleasing work for band and is quickly becoming a Canadian band classic.

This three-movement piece offers an enjoyable challenge to every section of the band. The nautical flavor of the first movement, *Downbound from Thunder Bay*, reflects the hustle and bustle of Great Lakes transportation. The lyrical trumpet solo in the second movement, *Point Pelee*, evokes images of a quiet stroll through the Point Pelee bird sanctuary on the shores of Lake Erie. The final movement, *Old Fort Henry*—a traditional British full-dress march reminiscent of Victorian Upper Canada—can also be programmed to stand alone: perfect for an encore.

Howard Cable writes of *Ontario Pictures:*

Each of the three pictures began with mental images and sense perceptions.

I have had a lifelong fascination with the lore of the Great Lakes. On becoming principal guest conductor of the Thunder Bay Symphony (Thunder Bay is on Lake Superior), I was at the lake head often and had many opportunities to dock walk and to talk with shipmates and crewmen. I learned much about the traditions, the trade, and the history of Great Lakes shipping, and the writing came quickly thereafter. There is an irony in the fact that the piece began at a time when this mode of transportation was rapidly becoming obsolete.

At Point Pelee one can find the quiet calm that leads to a oneness with nature, and there are millions of birds to give the tranquility a twinkle. It is the perfectly peaceful place, and that is what dictates the form. The joining of sunlit, multi-colored foliage with shining water suggested a warm afternoon solo trumpet, surrounded by woodwind filigree. (This piece is published separately as a trumpet solo with band and piano.)

To be inside Old Fort Henry in Kingston is to return to the past century and to feel the frontier as it was around 1840. That is the year my great-great-grandfather was stationed there with the British Army. When I am at the Fort, I sense the military traditions of Queen Victoria's time, and in the March I have tried to capture the feel of the Empire 100 years ago. History tells us that the Fort maintained the alert, ready to repulse an invader—who never came.

(Keith Kinder, interview with the composer, and Northdale Music Press, used by permission)

The last movement of the concert band version has been recorded by the University of Toronto Wind Symphony on a CD entitled *Wind Symphony* (Arbordisc UTWS 9701).

Québec Folk Fantasy
Difficulty: Grade 5
Duration: 7:00
Published 1956 by Chappell (out of print)
Available through CMC (www.musiccentre.ca)

This extraordinary setting for winds is based on some ten Québec folk songs, many of which are quite familiar while others are less well known. Sections based on each tune flow smoothly one to the next through skillful modulations and transitions based on fragments of the tunes themselves. This level of compositional integration, along with outstanding scoring, has made this work a favorite of Canadian band directors. (CMC and Keith Kinder)

A recording of this work is available on the CD "Dreaming on the 2238," (Arbordisc UTWS 9501) by the University of Toronto Wind Symphony.

Saskatchewan Overture
Difficulty: Grade 3.5
Duration: 5:30
Published 2007 by Eighth Note Publications (www.enpmusic.com)

Saskatchewan Overture was commissioned by The Saskatoon Concert Band. "Saskatchewan" is the Cree word meaning, "river that flows swiftly." In fact, the Cree River flows through the far northern reaches of Saskatchewan. In the mid 19th century Saskatchewan was a vast, flat, treeless and lawless area. By contrast, in the 21st century it is a vibrant energetic blend of wheat, oil, potash and gas production. It was the composer's goal to capture in music that forward thrust and the rhythmic pulse of the province today. (© Eighth Note Publications, used by permission)

Scene in Iqaluit
Difficulty: Grade 2
Duration: 2:50
Published 2007 by Eighth Note Publications (www.enpmusic.com)

With the announcement that a Royal visit was scheduled to Nunavut in October of 2002, The Iqaluit Music Society commissioned Mr. Cable to compose a work that would be idiomatic to Nunavut and reflect the culture. The performance would take place on the first day of the visit by H.R.H. Elizabeth II and would be played by the Inuksuk High School Band. The motif on which the work is based is an Inuit scale. A full percussion section is essential in order to properly reflect the culture. (© Eighth Note Publications, used by permission)

Scottish Rhapsody
Difficulty: Grade 5
Duration: 8:45
Published 2000 by Northdale Music Press (www.northdalemusic.com)

Scottish Rhapsody, out of print for many years, has now been reissued, complete with the full conductor's score (never before available). Cable's particular gift for a warm, rich, and full instrumentation is immediately evident in his tuneful, celebratory salute to the songs of Scottish poet Robert Burns. This skillful compilation of Scottish folk songs is Cable at his best – embracing the melodies in ways that skillfully bring out the diverse range of tones and textures that the concert band is capable of producing.

The composer writes, "The inspiration for writing *Scottish Rhapsody* came from listener reaction to a Cable Concert Band broadcast. It was New Year's Day and I described *Hogmanay* and *Auld Lang Syne* and mentioned that I was a Nairn on my mother's side. Letters came in from Scots suggesting that I 'Tak' a right gude willy waught' (a hearty drink as described in the 4th verse of *Auld Lang Syne*), reflect on my ancestors and write a celebratory salute to the great poet Robert Burns. The work was completed in time to premiere on a 'Burns Night' broadcast by the Cable Concert Band the following year." The work is subtitled *A Rhapsody on the Songs of Robbie Burns (1759–1776)*, and contains the following Scottish folk tunes: *A Man's a Man for A' That; Robin Adair; Ca' the Yowes to the Knowes; Comin' Through the Rye; A Red, Red Rose, Green Grow the Rashes, O; The Banks o' Doon*; and *Scots Wha Hae*. (Interview with the composer and Northdale Music Press, used by permission)

A pedagogical discussion of this work can be found on page 106 of *Canadian Music: A Selective Guidelist for Teachers* by Patricia Martin Shand.

Snake Fence Country: *a rural holiday*
Difficulty: Grade 5
Duration: 6:11
Published 1955 by Chappell (out of print)
Available through CMC (www.musiccentre.ca)

The title refers to pioneer rail fences built in a zigzag pattern, which once were a common sight in many parts of Canada and the United States. This piece is modeled on a country dance in which the musicians would present a continuous flow of songs to keep the dancers on the floor. The three dance melodies used here, *Buffalo Gals, Red River Valley*, and *Turkey in the Straw*, all have a distinctly rural flavor and both Canadian and American origins. This bright, cheerful music, with a lilting dance tempo throughout, is challenging to play, but exciting listening for performers and audience alike. It is comparable both in flavor and quality to Robert Russell Bennett's *Suite of Old American Dances*, and could easily substitute for that work in a pops concert. (CMC and Keith Kinder)

A recording of this work is available on the CD "McIntyre Ranch Country – Songs of the West," by the Lethbridge Community Gold Band, and may be ordered from their website, www.lcbs.ca/index.html.

Stratford Suite: Four Shakespearean Scenes for Concert Band
Difficulty: Grade 6
Duration: 13:00
Published 1964 by Chappell (out of print)

This brilliantly scored suite of four movements was commissioned by the Goldman Band to celebrate the 300th anniversary of Shakespeare's birth. It was premiered by the Goldman Band, Richard Franko Goldman, conducting, in New York's Prospect Park on June 20, 1964. Cable's skillful scoring displays his ability as a 20th century composer to convey the atmosphere of a Shakespearean play. Although the *Stratford Suite* is out of print, it may still be found in many established libraries. The quality of the work would more than justify a search.

The first movement, *Fanfare, Flourish, Sennet,* is written for brass and percussion and evokes the mood of the royal court as portrayed in *Richard III.* A scene from the *Merry Wives of Windsor* is the musical intent of the second movement, *Masque by Herne's Oak.* The third movement, *Ode to Rosalind,* employs only the woodwinds and percussion, and is identified with *As You Like It.* The majestic style of the final movement, *Elizabeth, Princess of England,* is suggestive of a scene from *Henry VIII.* Those wishing to program this out of print work may find it in the library of a nearby university or a high school with an older collection. (CMC, New York Times, and interview with the composer)

A pedagogical discussion of this work can be found on page 107 of *Canadian Music: A Selective Guidelist for Teachers* by Patricia Martin Shand.

MORLEY CALVERT (1928–1991)

MORLEY CALVERT WAS A conductor, bandmaster and composer born in Brantford, Ontario, and received his bachelor of music degree from McGill in 1956. In 1958, Calvert founded the Monteregian Music Camp (providing summer training for high school students) at Ayers Cliff, Montreal, a camp that ended in 1970. He founded and directed the McGill University Concert Band, as well as starting a high school band in Montreal at Westmount High School. In 1967–72, Calvert founded and directed the Lakeshore Concert Band in Montreal.

Calvert's professional activities included the position of accompanist for contralto Maureen Forrester, Canada's grande dame of song and one of Canada's musical ambassadors to the world. Calvert was invited to join the American Bandmasters Association, and taught the high school band program at Barrie Central Collegiate School. He was President of the Ontario Chapter of the Canadian Bandmasters Association, and from 1981–83, Executive Vice-President of the National Chapter of the Canadian Bandmasters Association. He was the artistic director of the Civic Concert Choir of Hamilton in 1987, and of the Weston Silver Band in 1988.

He composed and arranged works for band (some of which were for the Salvation Army), for brass quintet and for choir. His *Suite for the Monteregian Hills* for brass quintet, published in 1961 by Berandol, was based on French Canadian folk songs and was named for the mountain range stretching from Mount Royal, Québec to the American border. Many of his compositions employ folk music material and are light, pleasing works. At the time of his death, he was teaching music at Mohawk College in Hamilton, Ontario. (CMC, The Canadian Encyclopedia, and www.classical-composers.org)

Romantic Variations
Difficulty: Grade 4
Duration: 9:00
Published 1979 by G.V. Thompson (out of print)
Available through CMC (www.musiccentre.ca)

Commissioned in 1975 by the Youth Band of Ontario, *Romantic Variations* is an elegant, lyrical work in a Romantic style reminiscent of Tchaikovsky. The original theme in the clarinets is followed by six variations that alternate between lyrical and lively. The clarinets are featured throughout, with low, lyrical passages and some difficulty in performance beyond technical considerations. This is a significant work that depends on flowing lyricism, and a flowing line with light accompaniment is essential. This work provides an excellent opportunity to perform an original work for band in a 19th century idiom. (Jeff Reynolds)

Suite on Canadian Folk Songs
Difficulty: Grade 4
Duration: 10:00
Published 2006 by Eighth Note Publications (www.enpmusic.com)

Suite on Canadian Folk Songs originally was written as a Canadian Centennial project in 1967 for brass band. Until this edition, the concert band version remained unpublished, although it has attracted the admiration of many band directors.

This masterfully written suite is in three movements, the first and last being arrangements of French Canadian folk songs, and the middle movement an arrangement of a song from Newfoundland. 1. *Marianne s'es va-t-au Moulin* is the story of a young girl who went to the mill to grind some grain. While she was there her donkey was eaten by a wolf. This movement is an energetic allegro in 6/8 meter. 2. The Dorian love song *She's Like the Swallow* is typical of the slow-melody folk songs of the island province of Newfoundland. Quarter note = 88 in 3/4 meter in this movement, which is more expressive and cantabile in style. 3. *J'entends le Moulin* (I Hear the Mill) from Québec is in the form of three variations. It begins at quarter note = 120, with the intensity and tempo of the movement increasing with each variation and concluding in a swirling frenzy. (Jeff Reynolds, Patricia Shand, and Eighth Note Publications, used by permission)

A pedagogical discussion of this work can be found on page 10 of *Guidelist of Unpublished Canadian Band Music Suitable for Student Performers* by Patricia Martin Shand.

A recording of this work is available on the CD "A Lakeshore Concert," by the Lakeshore Concert Band of Montreal, and may be ordered by emailing the band at *lakeshoreconcertband@coolgoose.com*.

BRUCE CARLSON (B. 1944)

BRUCE CARLSON STUDIED THEORY and harmony initially in Toronto with Captain W.T. Atkins, conductor of the Queen's Own Rifles Band, and composition in Winnipeg with Dr. Robert Turner, one of Canada's best-known composers. He graduated from the University of Waterloo (B.A., 1967), University of Toronto (Teaching Certificate, 1969), and the University of Manitoba (Music, 1974).

Since 1975, he has received numerous commissions through the Manitoba Arts Council to write for the Music Inter Alia and Aurora Musicale concert series, the University of Manitoba, the City of Winnipeg, various professional and amateur choirs and professional musicians. His works have been broadcast frequently over the CBC on numerous programs and have been performed by the Festival Quartet of Canada, The Winnipeg Brass, The Winnipeg Singers, the Winnipeg Philharmonic Choir, the Purcell String Quartet, numerous amateur and professional choirs and various professional chamber ensembles. His *Chronlyricles I* for flute and lute opened a petroglyph display at the Museum of Man and Nature in Winnipeg in 1981. Numerous anthems published by his own company, Dox, have been performed throughout North America and Europe. He has been involved with three other composers in a new music concert series that provides a forum for performing their own music.

Various critics of the Winnipeg Free Press have described Carlson's music in the following manner: "...carries the listener from bar to bar with reassuring logic and artistry," "an intense lyrical emotional experience," "unpretentious, warm-hearted pieces," "this delicately interwoven music proved graceful, inventive and engaging," "a gifted and accomplished composer with a broad range."

He was awarded a major arts grant in 1981 and a short-term grant in 1988 by the Manitoba Arts Council. Presently he is the supervisor of the School of Music library as well as a part-time lecturer at the School of Music at the University of Manitoba. His professional affiliations include the Composers, Authors and Publishers Association of Canada, Canadian League of Composers, and the Manitoba Composers Association. (CMC)

Toledo
Difficulty: Grade 3
Duration: 9:40
Composed in 1992
Published by Dox Music
Available through CMC (www.musiccentre.ca)

Bruce Carlson's *Toledo* was commissioned in 1992 through the Manitoba Arts Council by the Henderson Junior High School Wind Ensemble, Jeff Kula, conductor. The work draws on compositional techniques developed during the late 20th century, including improvisation, aleatoric structure, time controlled by seconds rather than strict rhythm, and a strong interest in timbre and texture, especially percussion sounds.

Toledo was inspired by three related sources: the famous painting "View of Toledo" by El Greco; the "Spiritual Canticle" by St. John of the Cross; and the ruminations on both of the above by the Christian monk, Thomas Merton. Merton was the first to observe that while El Greco was painting "View of Toledo," St. John of the Cross was imprisoned in the city itself. These two artistic works emerged simultaneously but take very different views of spirituality. El Greco's perspective is dramatic and stormy, a glimpse of the end of the world, whereas the view of St. John of the Cross is marked by stillness and serenity. In *Toledo,* Carlson has attempted to reflect both of these concepts. He requests that a slide of "View of Toledo" be displayed above the band during the performance. At one point the players discuss the painting verbally and musically through improvisation. This striking work presents limited technical challenges, but it grows out of the rich history of musical development in the 20th century, and attempts to address profound spiritual concerns. (CMC and Keith Kinder)

CHAN KA NIN (B. 1949)

CHAN KA NIN WAS born in Hong Kong and moved with his family to Vancouver, BC in 1965. At the University of British Columbia he studied composition with Jean Coulthard while pursuing a Bachelor's degree in Electrical Engineering. After graduation he decided to continue studying composition with Bernhard Heiden at Indiana University, where he eventually obtained his Master's and Doctoral degrees in music. Since 1982 he has taught theory and composition at the University of Toronto.

Chan Ka Nin's works have been performed by professional ensembles throughout Canada, twice winning JUNO Awards for Best Classical Composition. His numerous international awards include the Jean Chalmers Award, Béla Bartók International Composers' Competition, Barlow International Competitions, International Horn Society Composition Contest, PROCAN Young Composers' Competition and Amherst Saxophone Quartet Composition Competition. (CMC and Jeff Reynolds)

Ecstasy
Difficulty: Grade 5
Duration: 10:00
Available through CMC (www.musiccentre.ca)

Ecstasy, originally composed for chamber orchestra, was written in 1987 on a commission from the Esprit Orchestra of Toronto, a professional chamber orchestra conducted by Alex Pauk that performs only music of the past 50 years. The composer rewrote it for band a year later, but the band version is more than a simple transcription. A number of revisions were made to ensure that the music was well suited to its new medium. Of the work, the composer has said that he was inspired by the various states of ecstasy, from personal contemplation to public rejoicing: "The first inspiration of the piece came as a feeling of rushing jubilation. Later other aspects, such as the quiet feeling of ecstasy one might feel in communion with nature, came to mind, and these too are reflected in the music."

The work opens dramatically with a pyramid consisting of multiple octaves of the single pitch "E" rising swiftly through the ensemble, and leading to a group of rapid melodic figures at a very fast tempo. This dramatic music is quickly replaced by restrained lyrical passages, many of which feature solo textures. The composer restricted himself to the seven notes of a diatonic scale, apparently to employ the simplest means to represent the many kinds of ecstatic experience. However, while the musical means may be restricted, their use is anything but simplistic. Chan has built all his melodic material from five-note groupings that sound pentatonic and recall Chinese music. The piece is also complex rhythmically, with different levels of superimposed subdivision. Intriguing timbral blends, such as bass clarinet and piccolo, draw skillfully on the resources of the wind band. *Ecstasy* is a moving and exciting composition that comprises a fine amalgam of Eastern and Western traditions, and stands on its own as an excellent addition to the repertoire. (CMC and Keith Kinder)

Memento Mori
Difficulty: Grade 6
Duration: 23:00
Composed in 1998
Available through CMC (www.musiccentre.ca)

Memento Mori was commissioned for the Edmonton Symphony by the Canadian Broadcasting Corporation in 1998, and was rescored in 2003 for wind ensemble. The note in the score reads, in part: "*Memento Mori* means something that serves as a reminder of death. In Latin, it is translated as 'Remember that you must die.' The two meanings appeal to the composer because the first explanation relates to humans and how they deal with death; the second relates to nature—that a life cycle must come to an end. His dark as well as celebratory responses to this theme are evident at different levels in this multi-movement work. The sustained tone is a constant reminder of man's ultimate fate, while the repeated notes symbolize something that is eternal. He would like to dedicate this work to all who suffer."

Solemn, brooding and nostalgic sections are contrasted with youthful, lyrical and glorious passages. The three movements are played without pause, and strong woodwind soloists are required. The percussion section is featured throughout, from timpani, marimba, glockenspiel and crotales, to more exotic instruments such as Chinese bend-up gong, waterphone, and, in the composer's words, "as many nipple-gongs and exotic gongs as you can find." This work requires a highly capable ensemble. (CMC and Jeff Reynolds)

STEPHEN CHATMAN (B. 1950)

STEPHEN CHATMAN, PROFESSOR AND Head of the Composition Division at The University of British Columbia, Vancouver since 1976, studied with Joseph Wood and Walter Aschaffenburg at the Oberlin Conservatory and with Ross Lee Finney, Leslie Bassett, William Bolcom, and Eugene Kurtz at the University of Michigan in Ann Arbor. He completed his D.M.A. degree in 1977.

Stylistically, many of Chatman's pre-1982 works are complex, virtuosic, and atonal. His early chamber works, in particular, are highly concerned with color, contrast, and tightly controlled motivic development. In 1982, Chatman began composing choral music influenced by various traditional musical styles. *You Have Ravished My Heart* for SATB (1982), a transitional work and the first of many "accessible" or "popular" choral works, signals Chatman's gradual departure from modernism and a path toward post-modernism, spirituality, and a wider audience. These post-1982 secular and sacred choral works, in addition to many educational piano pieces, embrace a predominantly pan-diatonic tonal language, lyricism, melody, folk song, and more traditional musical gestures, forms, and compositional techniques.

In 1988–89, Chatman became British Columbia's first "composer in residence," composing several works for Vancouver's Music in the Morning concert series, June Goldsmith, director. He also was composer in residence with the National Youth Orchestra of Canada in 2004. In 2003, Chatman was one of three Canadian composers to visit Beijing and Shanghai in the "First Exchange of Canadian and Chinese Composers," sponsored by the Chinese Musicians' Association and the Consulate General of the People's Republic of China in Vancouver. In 2004, he was the first composer ever awarded the Dorothy Somerset Award for Performance and Development in the Visual and Creative Arts from the University of British Columbia.

The only North American to have won three consecutive BMI Awards to Student Composers, Inc. (New York) prizes (1974, '75, '76), Chatman has also received a Charles Ives Scholarship from the American Academy of Arts and Letters, an M.B. Rockefeller Fund Grant, and a U.S. Fulbright Grant for study with Karlheinz Stockhausen at the Hochschule fur Musik in Cologne.

Winner of the 2005 Western Canadian Music Awards "Outstanding Classical Composition" for *Proud Music of the Storm,* he is the first Canadian ever short-listed in the BBC Masterprize international competition (2001, *Tara's Dream* for orchestra). His orchestral works, commissioned by the Vancouver, Toronto, Edmonton, Windsor, and Madison symphonies and the CBC Radio Orchestra have been performed and recorded by numerous symphonies around the world, and his piano music is included in the syllabus of Canada's Royal Conservatory of Music.

As Professor of composition and orchestration, co-director of University of British Columbia Contemporary Players new music ensemble, and Head of the

UBC School of Music composition division, Chatman has taught a generation of prominent Canadian composers. Chatman, who has served on many Canada Council juries and national student composition contest juries, was Jury Chairman of the 2001 CBC National Radio Competition for Young Composers. He is an Associate Composer of the Canadian Music Centre, a past President of Vancouver New Music; and a member of the Canadian League of Composers, the Society of Composers, Authors and Music Publishers of Canada (SOCAN), the Society of Composers, Inc., and the American Music Center. (CMC, The Canadian Encyclopedia, and Eighth Note Publications, used by permission)

Grouse Mountain Lullaby
Difficulty: Grade 2
Duration: 2:55
Published by Hal Leonard

Grouse Mountain, a popular ski resort, overlooks the composer's home city of Vancouver, B.C. This gentle music in 3/4 time is a nocturne reminiscent of Eric Satie's piano works, and is well suited to performance by a young band. (Fraser Linklater)

A recording of this work is available on the CD "North Winds—Canadian Wind Band Music," which may be ordered from the University of Manitoba, Faculty of Music, 65 Dafoe Road, Winnipeg, Manitoba, Canada R3T 2N2 or by calling (204) 474-9310.

Mountain Sojourn
Difficulty: Grade 3
Duration: 5:30
Published 2004 by Eighth Note Publications (www.enpmusic.com)

This is the composer's orchestration of his choral work, *There is Sweet Music Here*. The joyous outer movements, *Song of the Laughing Green Woods* and *Piping Down the Valley's Wild*, inspired by William Blake's *Songs of Innocence*, show the influence of the early twentieth century English tradition. The gentler, more reflective middle movement, *Softer Falls Than Petals*, is inspired by Alfred Tennyson's *There is Sweet Music Here*. (© Eighth Note Publications, used by permission)

Walnut Grove Suite
Difficulty: Grade 3
Duration: 5:50
Published 2004 by Eighth Note Publications (www.enpmusic.com)

Commissioned by the Walnut Grove Secondary School in Langley, B.C, this suite opens with *Fraser River Fanfare*, which reflects the treacherous western Canadian river. In the second movement, entitled *A Swallow in the Valley*, the folk song *She's Like the Swallow* is the source. *Fort Langley March,* rounding out this work, is written in the tradition of early twentieth century military band marches. The work as a whole contains some unusual harmonic twists that enhance its interest. (© Eighth Note Publications, used by permission)

DONALD COAKLEY (B. 1934)

ONE OF THE MOST prolific and highly respected of all Canadian composers, Donald Coakley is a native of Preston (now Cambridge, Ontario). He studied at the Crane School of Music at the State University of New York in Potsdam, New York, the School of Music at Temple University, and the Philadelphia Conservatory of Music. While studying at the Conservatory he was a composition student of Vincent Persichetti and trombone student of Henry Charles Smith, principal trombone of the Philadelphia Orchestra. Following graduate school, he taught at Cardinal Dougherty High School in Philadelphia, and also served as conductor of the Camden Choral Arts Society in Camden, New Jersey. After a successful tenure at Cardinal Dougherty, Coakley joined the faculty of the School of Music at Temple University.

In the early 1970's, Coakley was invited to join the Music Department of the Scarborough School System, becoming Assistant Coordinator of Music shortly thereafter. As such, he was responsible for the elementary instrumental music program in the school system for 22 years. He also headed the instrumental wing at the Scarborough Music Camps. In 1970 he founded the Scarborough Schools Symphony Orchestra and subsequently oversaw the inception of four other All-City instrumental ensembles. Following his retirement from the Scarborough Board of Education, Coakley was for six years conductor of the York University Symphonic Band.

Coakley is well known for his work as a composer. He has written extensively for band, orchestra, choir and chamber ensemble. Although he has written successfully for many groups, both amateur and professional, his major effort has been dedicated to music for school groups. He is a member of the Canadian League of Composers, as well as an Associate Composer with the Canadian Music Centre. In 1977 Coakley received the Distinguished Service to Education Award from the State University of New York; and in 1994 he received the Anson Taylor Award for excellence in teaching from the Scarborough Board of Education. In addition to his activities as a composer, Coakley has been, for the past ten years, an avid student of classical drawing and painting, and a passionate landscape painter. (Interview with the composer, CMC, and Eighth Note Publications, used by permission)

Antiphonals
Difficulty: Grade 4
Duration: 7:00
Composed in 2000
Available through the composer (email dcoakley@sympatico.ca)

Antiphonals follows the form and style of *Canzon Septimi Toni No. 2*, written by Giovanni Gabrieli during the rich artistic and musical period of the High

Renaissance. In that sense, this work makes use of antiphonal effects between the woodwind, brass and percussion sections of the band. Also, in the style of Gabrielli, this composition makes abundant use of polyphony. The work was commissioned by the Barrie North Collegiate Institute Concert Band. (Interview with the composer)

Bonavist Harbour
Difficulty: Grade 3
Duration: 3:30
Published 2007 by Eighth Note Publications (www.enpmusic.com)

Bonavist Harbour is based on a catchy folk tune popular in Newfoundland. A shorter version, often sung by Newfoundlanders, is known as "The Feller From Fortune." Both versions are rollicking and good humored. The refrain and verses are full of nonsense lyrics. The work is strong and vigorous, and is marked "with gusto." The composer has written extensive notes to the conductor in the score. (© Eighth Note Publications, used by permission)

Bright Blue Water
Difficulty: Grade 3
Duration: 7:10
Published 2004 by Eighth Note Publications (www.enpmusic.com)

This substantial work was commissioned by Mowat Collegiate Institute in Scarborough, Ontario, to celebrate its 25th anniversary. The driving rhythms, plentiful percussion and melodic material make this work an excellent choice for either concert or contest use. The rich, legato middle section, in a dark warm key, is framed by energetic fast sections with many changes in meter. (© Eighth Note Publications, used by permission)

A Canadian Folk Rhapsody
Difficulty: Grade 4
Duration: 5:20
Published 2004 by Eighth Note Publications (www.enpmusic.com)

Woven within *A Canadian Folk Rhapsody* are four folk melodies chosen for their potential to interact successfully within the bounds of a single composition. They are part of the cultural heritage of the two principal ethnic groups that populate Canada—French and English. The melodies are mostly in triple meter and are from different regions of the country.

The work is focused around *Flunky Jim*, a song written in Saskatchewan during the Great Depression, which describes a young man's plans for new clothing paid for by collecting the bounty on gophers. Contrasting with this vigorous song is a lovely setting of *A la Claire Fontaine* in two verses. The third song is *Squid Jigging Ground*, a lively fishing song from Newfoundland with a humorous text that makes fun of politicians and wealthy people. *En roulant ma boule* is a very old song that originated in medieval times. An energetic dance tune, very popular in Québec, it is essentially a children's fairy tale. These four songs complement each other well, making the *Rhapsody* an enjoyable work with considerable musical variety. (Interview with the composer and Eighth Note Publications, used by permission)

Cantos
Difficulty: Grade 4
Duration: 4:00
Published 1998 by Eighth Note Publications (www.enpmusic.com)

The title *Cantos* derives from that form of poetry in which a poem, in most cases epic in nature, consists of many short verses. There are four contrasting movements: *Prologue,* fast and lively in 2/4 time, with a short lyrical woodwind passage as the center; *Interlude,* lyrical and slow, featuring an oboe solo (cued in flute); *Dance,* moderato featuring timpani, bassoon, and piccolo; and *Epilogue,* allegro featuring piccolo and xylophone in an asymmetrical rhythmic setting. All are very short and contain interesting material for all players. Soloistic playing, asymmetrical meters, and unconventional melodies make this work an excellent teaching piece. The composer wrote *Cantos* in the 1970's, and this new edition is fully edited and features some altered sections. (Jeff Reynolds and Eighth Note Publications, used by permission)

A pedagogical discussion of this work can be found on page 110 of *Canadian Music: A Selective Guidelist for Teachers* by Patricia Martin Shand.

Canzona
Difficulty: Grade 4
Duration: 6:00
Composed in 1985
Available through the composer (email dcoakley@sympatico.ca)

Canzona was commissioned by the Birchmount Collegiate Institute Concert Band in Scarborough, Ontario, and is based on the instrumental canzonas of the late sixteenth century. While the tempo is fairly fast, the melodic material, in the spirit of the vocal as well as instrumental canzonas of that time period, is lyrical in style. *Canzona* also follows sixteenth century form, with a contrasting middle section followed by a re-statement of the opening material. A brief coda brings the work to a close. (Interview with the composer)

Celebration
Difficulty: Grade 3
Duration: 3:30
Published 1998 by Eighth Note Publications (www.enpmusic.com)

Composed with rhythmic and melodic interest, this work was originally the finale to a divertimento for strings. The tuneful melody is passed throughout the ensemble, and even low woodwinds and tubas have a short section of melody. Percussion parts animate driving rhythms and elegant writing in the winds. (© Eighth Note Publications, used by permission)

Declarative Statements, A Short Symphony for Band
Difficulty: Grade 6
Duration: 17:00
Composed in 1979
Available through the composer (email dcoakley@sympatico.ca)

Declarative Statements was commissioned by the University of Toronto Concert Band through a grant from the Ontario Arts Council. The work is based on an eleven bar opening section, played by the trumpets and trombones, along with percussion. What follows are six variations on the opening eleven bar statement. The variations are divided into two larger sections. The variants consist of fast and slow sections, along with aleatoric writing. The sixth variation leads to a brief coda, which brings the work to a close. This is a demanding work for the symphonic band. (Interview with the composer)

A Distant Voice
Difficulty: Grade 3.5
Duration: 9:30
Published 2007 by Eighth Note Publications (www.enpmusic.com)

This work was commissioned by Donald McKellar, Professor Emeritus of Music Education and Director of Bands at the Don Wright Faculty of Music, University of Western Ontario. He was founding chairman of the music education department, and enjoyed a long and distinguished career in the field of music education in Canada. He commissioned *A Distant Voice* following his retirement from the University. This work has no programmatic content, and was designed as a slow, reflective and stately composition. Throughout, *A Distant Voice* should be interpreted in a broad, reflective manner. A legato style throughout the composition is mandatory. Two contrasting melodies dominate. The work ends as it started, on a quiet, meditative note. (© Eighth Note Publications, used by permission)

Donkey Riding
Difficulty: Grade 2
Duration: 2:35
Published 1998 by Eighth Note Publications (www.enpmusic.com)

This famous folksong is an old sailors' song that originated on ships that sailed from Glasgow, Scotland and Liverpool, England to bring back timber from

Canada. It was sung as a work song to help the sailors load lumber onto the ships' decks. The melody is based on the Scottish march *Highland Laddie,* and the song was so widespread that a version of *Donkey Riding* was also sung by cotton stowers in Mobile, Alabama. The "donkey" in the title refers to the donkey engines, small steam engines, used in loading cargo onto the ships. The engine came to Canada via the port of Québec and was adopted by lumberjacks in the Ottawa Valley who used similar engines. Having such an engine allowed larger ships to be sailed by fewer crew, and today an auxiliary engine on a sailing craft is still sometimes informally known as "the donk." (Keith Kinder and Eighth Note Publications, used by permission)

A recording of this work is available on the CD "North Winds-Canadian Wind Band Music," which may be ordered from the University of Manitoba, Faculty of Music, 65 Dafoe Road, Winnipeg, Manitoba, Canada R3T 2N2 or by calling (204) 474-9310.

Elegaic Motives
Difficulty: Grade 3
Duration: 7:35
Published 2000 by Eighth Note Publications (www.enpmusic.com)

Elegiac Motives was commissioned by his parents in memory of a young man who died tragically at the beginning of his teenage years. The work is based on the tone row D-A-D-C-G-E, which are the note related letters in his name. Derivatives and harmonic material used in the work are generated from the row. This piece combines both a reflective feeling as well as sections of youthful energy. Members of the band have optional parts that can be sung. (© Eighth Note Publications, used by permission)

The Garnet and the Gold
Difficulty: Grade 3
Duration: 3:00
Published 2002 by Eighth Note Publications (www.enpmusic.com)

This exciting concert march is dedicated to Cardinal Dougherty High School in Philadelphia, Pennsylvania, where the composer was the Director of Bands for several years. The trio is based on the school's Alma Mater. Upper woodwind parts set in three-part harmony add special interest for the players. (© Eighth Note Publications, used by permission)

Gentle Clouds Roll By—A Chippewa Lullaby
Difficulty: Grade 2
Duration: 4:25
Published 2000 by Eighth Note Publications (www.enpmusic.com)

This lovely Chippewa lullaby was first collected on the western shores of the Great Lakes at the beginning of the twentieth century. The original "Way Way" text was obviously intended to gently lull a baby to sleep. Performing this work presents both the opportunity to perform with the school choir (or members of the band can sing the choral parts), and the option to work with the history department in the school when they are teaching about native peoples. Cross curriculum work is always popular and is of great benefit to students. (© Eighth Note Publications, used by permission)

Jubilant Dialogue
Difficulty: Grade 4
Duration: 6:30
Published 1998 by Eighth Note Publications (www.enpmusic.com)

Jubilant Dialogue was commissioned by Vincent Massey High School in Brandon, Manitoba, through a grant from the Canada Council. Dialogues between brass, woodwinds, and percussion take place throughout. Interesting percussion parts add to the power of the work. (© Eighth Note Publications, used by permission)

Land of the Silver Birch
Difficulty: Grade 1
Duration: 2:20
Published 2004 by Eighth Note Publications (www.enpmusic.com)

Land of the Silver Birch may be the quintessential Canadian folk song. The text is full of distinctively Canadian wilderness imagery, and the melody is supposedly Native Canadian, collected by 17th century Jesuit missionaries from the woodland tribes around the Great Lakes in Central Canada. It also was a well-known song in the summer camps of the region because of its evocation of the native peoples of North America. The haunting, mysterious quality of the melody from the Huron First Nations people is one of its most engaging features. Coakley's imaginative approach to motivic development has produced a musically rewarding arrangement of a tune familiar to all Canadian young people. (CMC, Keith Kinder, and Eighth Note Publications, used by permission)

A recording of this work is available on the CD "North Winds—Canadian Wind Band Music," which may be ordered from the University of Manitoba, Faculty of Music, 65 Dafoe Road, Winnipeg, Manitoba, Canada R3T 2N2 or by calling (204) 474-9310.

A pedagogical discussion of this work can be found on page 13 of *Guidelist of Unpublished Canadian Band Music Suitable for Student Performers* by Patricia Martin Shand.

Lyric Essay
Difficulty: Grade 3
Duration: 3:10
Published 2004 by Eighth Note Publications (www.enpmusic.com)

Since its composition in 1975, *Lyric Essay* has become a "Canadian classic," and is performed in Canada almost as often as works by Percy Grainger. It has attracted the interest of band directors at all levels and is probably Coakley's most performed composition.

Lyric Essay is written in a neo-romantic style. It is a gentle, reflective work with much opportunity for musical expression. This piece (previously published by E.C. Kirby) has been performed throughout Canada, the United States and in Japan. An ideal lyric composition to be programmed between two louder works, it consists of a single expressive melody that begins quietly, rises to a grand crescendo, and subsides to a peaceful ending. It is supported throughout by rich and unusual harmonies, and is an exceptional work to use in teaching expression. (CMC, Keith Kinder, and Eighth Note Publications, used by permission)

Lyric Essay has been recorded both by the University of Calgary Wind Ensemble and the Edmonton Wind Ensemble.

Masquerade
Difficulty: Grade 4
Duration: 13:50
Published 2007 by Eighth Note Publications (www.enpmusic.com)

Masquerade was commissioned by the Hannaford Street Silver Band, a British style brass band whose personnel is composed of members of the Opera and Ballet orchestras, as well as freelance musicians in Toronto, Ontario. The adaptation from brass band to concert band was written by the composer, who has included extensive notes to the conductor in the score. Desiring to personalize the work, Mr. Coakley created tone rows from the letter notes drawn from the names of the members of each section of the band. These individual rows were "boiled" down to one row and its derivatives. These four motives served as the thematic, and harmonic material for the composition. Masquerade is an apt title for the composition, since these elements come from the members of the band themselves. Combined with the row and derivatives, graphic, and improvisational techniques were used in constructing this piece. After a brief opening, in which elements of all the original rows are stated, ending in a complete statement of the "synthesized" row, seven variations on this final ordering of tones, and its derivatives follow. A brief, coda-like section brings the work to a conclusion. As stated, the title *Masquerade* seemed appropriate, since, without revealing identities, the members of the band are the composition. (© Eighth Note Publications, used by permission)

The Moon Reflected in Twin Ponds
Difficulty: Grade 3
Duration: 9:30
Published 2007 by Eighth Note Publications (www.enpmusic.com)

The Moon Reflected In Twin Ponds was commissioned for the Dr. Norman Bethune Collegiate Concert Band, in Toronto, Ontario, to celebrate the twenty-fifth anniversary of the school. This school has a large Chinese population, and membership in the senior band consists mostly of Chinese students. When Mr. Coakley was asked to take on the commission, it seemed fitting to write a work that spoke to the Chinese culture. As the basis for the commission, he chose an ancient Chinese folksong that speaks of tragedy and lost love.

This setting of the folksong makes no attempt to interpret the narrative. Rather, it uses the folksong to create a work that uses voices, graphic notation, and Chinese percussion instruments in its realization. The work is conceived in arch form, with reflective outer sections and many special affects achieved through singing, crystal glasses, glissandi, half valve tones, Chinese water gongs, and other percussion effects. The score includes extensive notes to the conductor to assist in achieving the effects the composer desires. (© Eighth Note Publications, used by permission)

Now the Morning is Begun: *A Festive Celebration*
Difficulty: Grade 3
Duration: 5:00
Published 2004 by Eighth Note Publications (www.enpmusic.com)

This celebratory work was commissioned by St. Michael's College School in Toronto to celebrate its 150th anniversary. It is constructed around two hymn tunes, *Hymn to St. Michael* and *Michael, Prince of all the Angels.* A strong, broad opening leads to a sustained middle section, and the fanfare ending is full and rich. (© Eighth Note Publications, used by permission)

Prelude on a Festive Hymn Tune
Difficulty: Grade 3
Duration: 3:30
Published 2004 by Eighth Note Publications (www.enpmusic.com)

Composer Donald Coakley was asked by the Pastor of St. William's Roman Catholic Church in Philadelphia, Pennsylvania to write a hymn based on verses he had written about the parish's namesake. What developed is this powerful and festive prelude. Fanfares in the trumpets, supportive ornamentation in the upper woodwinds, and melodic material throughout the ensemble make this an excellent choice for either concert or contest use. (© Eighth Note Publications, used by permission)

Prologue and Dramatic Music for Winds and Percussion
Difficulty: Grade 5
Duration: 12:00
Composed in 1980
Available through the composer (email dcoakley@sympatico.ca)

Prologue and Dramatic Music was commissioned by the Oakwood Collegiate Institute Wind Ensemble through a grant from the Ontario Arts Council. Percussion writing is very prominent in this work. The style of the composition, as the title implies, has a very strong dramatic component. An extended middle section using aleatoric writing for various sections of the wind ensemble leads to a re-statement of the opening material, which brings the work to a close. Like *Declarative Statements,* this work places real demands on the performers. (Interview with the composer)

A pedagogical discussion of this work can be found on page 44 of *Guidelist of Unpublished Canadian Band Music Suitable for Student Performers* by Patricia Martin Shand.

Regal Salute
Difficulty: Grade 1
Duration: 2:30
Published 2004 by Eighth Note Publications (www.enpmusic.com)

Regal Salute is a stately march in a processional style for young band. Strong melodic material, supported with a steady rhythmic feeling, propels this work. This would be an excellent first march for a young band. (© Eighth Note Publications, used by permission)

Songs for the Morning Band
Difficulty: Grade 2
Duration: 5:00
Composed in 1977
Published by E.C. Kerby

This work was a commission from the John Adaskan Project in Toronto. A grade two level composition in three movements, it follows the fast-slow-fast concept. This is an excellent work for introducing young players to contemporary harmony, simple meter changes, and a plethora of different articulations. The second movement is based on an Inuit melody that uses only 3 pitches, and yet Coakley's setting is quite expressive. Now distributed in North America by Hal Leonard, this is an excellent work for young band. (Keith Kinder and interview with the composer)

A recording of this work is available on the CD "North Winds—Canadian Wind Band Music," which may be ordered from the University of Manitoba, Faculty of Music, 65 Dafoe Road, Winnipeg, Manitoba, Canada R3T 2N2 or by calling (204) 474-9310.

Songs for the Morning Band
Difficulty: Grade 1.5
Duration: 5:00
Composed in 1977
Published 2007 by Eighth Note Publications (www.enpmusic.com)

This new publication of *Songs for the Morning Band* updates the original 1977 E.C. Kerby publication at a slightly more accessible grade level for young band. The first movement is entitled *The Answered Question,* a positive response to Charles Ives' *The Unanswered Question.* Throughout, this movement makes use of the question and answer technique. The second movement, *An Inuit Lullaby,* is a lyrical, legato setting of an old Inuit folksong from the Cape Dorset region of the Canadian Arctic. The third and final movement, *Entrance Of The Colourful Clowns,* is a depiction of circus clowns entering the center ring under the big tent of a circus. Like its 1977 predecessor, *Songs For the Morning Band* features contemporary harmonies, simple meter changes, and opportunities for expressive playing. The score offers notes to the conductor regarding interpretation of the piece. (© Eighth Note Publications, used by permission)

Sonics
Difficulty: Grade 6
Duration: 12:00
Published 1997 by Eighth Note Publications (www.enpmusic.com)

This piece, commissioned by the Markham District High School Wind Symphony, is a large-scale dramatic work for concert band. The first two measures contain the thematic structures that constitute the first, second, and closing themes. Chromatic harmonies and dissonant intervals create tension and excitement. Within the sonata-allegro form themes are introduced and developed throughout the ensemble. Contrapuntal elements as well as many meter changes (7/8, 5/8) keeps the pace of the piece quick and energetic. The composer describes this work as "acidy" and that term seems to best capture the mood of the piece. Professional and advanced bands may also consider this piece because of the virtuosity that is required from all players. (© Eighth Note Publications, used by permission)

Suite for a Band of Players
Difficulty: Grade 2
Duration: 9:00
Published 1995 by Jaymar
See description below.

A pedagogical discussion of this work can be found on page 15 of *Guidelist of Unpublished Canadian Band Music Suitable for Student Performers* by Patricia Martin Shand.

Suite for a Band of Players
Difficulty: Grade 1.5
Duration: 9:00
Published 2007 by Eighth Note Publications (www.enpmusic.com)

This new publication of *Suite For A Band Of Players* updates at a slightly easier grade level the original 1995 publication by Jaymar. It is a three-movement composition intended for students who have completed approximately two years of playing. The first movement, *Latino*, represents a synthesis of several Latin American rhythms, and is multi-metered to encourage the players to count carefully. If not enough percussionists are available to cover all the parts, players from other sections of the band could be used. The second movement, *D'ou Viens-tu, Bergere*, is a legato and lyrical folksong of French origin, popular in Quebec. The third movement, *Ritual Walk*, is a stately processional. All the movements utilize all the sections of the band, providing three interesting works for young musicians. (Interview with the composer)

Toccata Festiva
Difficulty: Grade 4
Duration: 6:00
Published 2002 by Eighth Note Publications (www.enpmusic.com)

Fanfares, declamatory passages, lyricism, memorable melodies and driving percussion parts are all found in this work. Like those early 17th century instrumental toccatas, *Toccata Festiva* has a strong celebratory character. *Toccata Festiva* is a work based on a medieval Gregorian Kyrie. Following the form of the Kyrie, this composition is in three sections. The Gregorian melody in the middle is scored for French horns, and is particularly beautiful. The work comes to an exciting finish. (Interview with the composer and Eighth Note Publications, used by permission)

A pedagogical discussion of this work can be found on page 46 of *Guidelist of Unpublished Canadian Band Music Suitable for Student Performers* by Patricia Martin Shand.

The Twentieth Century Band
Difficulty: Grade 2
Duration: 6:45
Published 1997 by Eighth Note Publications (www.enpmusic.com)

The Twentieth Century Band is the result of a commission from the Alliance for Canadian New Music Projects, with funding from the Ontario Arts Council. It offers young students a variety of traditional 20th century compositional techniques presented in an easy and accessible framework. It is designed to introduce young players to such devices as quartal and modal harmonies, polytonality, polymeter, and twelve-tone techniques. Each of the three movements, *Six in a Row, Modal Song,* and *Polymetrechordalcluster March,* present young performers with both musical and technical challenges. (The Canadian Encyclopedia and Eighth Note Publications, used by permission)

A pedagogical discussion of this work can be found on page 16 of *Guidelist of Unpublished Canadian Band Music Suitable for Student Performers* by Patricia Martin Shand.

Vive la Canadienne

Difficulty: Grade 5
Duration: 4:30
Published 1994 by Northdale Music Press (www.northdalemusic.com)

Vive la Canadienne is a national song that was most frequently sung in Québec before *O Canada* became popular. According to historian Marius Barbeau the words to the song probably were written by an oarsman. This arrangement of *Vive la Canadienne* is one of six compositions for concert band that premièred July 1, 1986 at the Canada and Ontario Pavilions at Expo 86 in Vancouver. The Northdale Concert Band, funded by the Ontario Arts Council, commissioned works by six composers to mark the International Year of Canadian Music.

Each composer was asked to create an entertaining piece appropriate for national and heritage events. The music provides melodic, festive, and accessible writing to foster an atmosphere of celebration. *Vive la Canadienne* is a vibrant toast to the Canadian girl, using as its melody the rousing traditional French Canadian chanson *Par derrièr' chez mon père.*

A spirited work in one movement based on the traditional French Canadian folk tune, this work features rapid technical passages in the upper winds and requires a solid bottom as well as a fearless trombone section. *Vive la Canadienne* should be played with a sense of brilliance and flair. Throughout the composition, Coakley treats this tune with lively brass fanfares, brilliant woodwind flourishes, and imaginative variations, bringing the work to an exciting and colorful conclusion. An excellent concert opener or closer, this tune is familiar to every Canadian. (The Canadian Encyclopedia, interview with the composer, and Northdale Music Press, used by permission)

Vive la Canadienne has been recorded by the University of Toronto Wind Symphony on a CD entitled *Dreaming on the 2238* (Arbordisc UTWS 9501). A recording of this work also is available on the CD "A Lakeshore Concert," by the Lakeshore Concert Band of Montreal, and may be ordered by emailing the band at *lakeshoreconcertband@coolgoose.com.*

MICHAEL COLGRASS (B. 1932)

MICHAEL COLGRASS STARTED HIS musical career at age 12 with his own jazz band. Only when he went to the University of Illinois in 1954 did he enter the world of symphonic music, first as a percussionist and then as composer. After composition studies with Lukas Foss and Darius Milhaud at the Berkshire Music Festival and the Aspen School, Colgrass went to New York and free-lanced with a wide range of groups, including the New York Philharmonic, Dizzy Gillespie, the original West Side Story orchestra on Broadway, the Columbia Recording Orchestra's Stravinsky Conducts Stravinsky series, and numerous ballet, opera and jazz ensembles. During this time he continued to study composition with Wallingford Riegger and Ben Weber.

As a percussion soloist he premiered many of his own works. In 1967 he stopped playing to devote himself entirely to composing. Since then he has received commissions from the New York Philharmonic, The Boston Symphony Orchestra, the Toronto Symphony Orchestra, the National Arts Centre Orchestra, The Minnesota Orchestra, the Canadian Broadcasting Corporation, The Lincoln Center Chamber Music Society, and numerous other orchestras, chamber groups, choral groups, soloists and organizations.

He won the 1978 Pulitzer Prize for Music for *Déjà vu*, which was commissioned and premiered by the New York Philharmonic. In addition, he received an Emmy Award in 1982 for a PBS documentary "Soundings: The Music of Michael Colgrass." He has been awarded two Guggenheim Fellowships, A Rockefeller Grant, First Prize in the Barlow and Sudler International Wind Ensemble Competitions, and the 1988 Jules Leger Prize for Chamber Music.

Although he makes his living as a composer, he has for 25 years presented workshops throughout North America in performing excellence, combining Grotowski physical training, mime, dance and Neuro-Linguistic Programming (NLP). He has given workshops in the United States, Canada, England, Ireland, Italy, Indonesia, South Africa, Argentina, Uruguay and Brazil. His teaching techniques were featured in the PBS documentary, "Soundings: The Music of Michael Colgrass" and also in his recently completed book, *My Lessons with Kumi—How I Learned to Perform with Confidence in Life and Work*. His strategies for creativity are explained in Robert Dilts' book *Tools For Dreamers*. He is the founder of Deep Listening, a technique for using hypnosis with audiences to enhance listening pleasure, which is featured in the book of outstanding NLP developments, *Leaves Before The Wind*.

Colgrass has written much music for children and recently initiated music creativity projects in middle schools in Toronto, and Longmeadow, Massachusetts. He is currently active in networking the activities of music-loving parents and teachers throughout North America who have successfully fought to save music programs in their schools when threatened by cutbacks.

He lives in Toronto and makes his living internationally as a composer. His wife, Ulla, is a journalist and editor who writes about music and the arts. (CMC and the composer's website, www.michaelcolgrass.com)

Apache Lullaby
Difficulty: Grade 1
Duration: 4:45
Published 2003 by Colgrass Music

As a result of his composition *Old Churches,* Pulitzer Prize-winning composer Michael Colgrass was invited to participate in a residency and composition workshop with the Longmeadow, Massachusetts, School District in fall 2003. Colgrass's visit was the result of a grant from the nonprofit Longmeadow Educational Excellence Foundation. The result of his residency, *Apache Lullaby*, is an example of divided part writing, where not all of the instruments play the same thing at the same time. Even a single section, such as the clarinets, will be divided into two or three parts. The sound is immediately recognizable as more complicated and having more texture.

Based on a lullaby that Colgrass heard an Apache mother sing to her child, this lyric piece for beginning band is a series of variations on the melody, capturing different moods of native Indian life, from tranquil, to mysterious to heroic. Different sections of the ensemble are featured in each variation, with easy counterpoint being introduced to the young musicians in a natural and attractive musical setting. The composer's intention in writing this work was to develop confidence in young performers.

Apache Lullaby was premiered by Chris Unczur conducting the Glenbrook Middle School Concert band in a concert at the Longmeadow High School in Longmeadow, Massachusetts, on December 11, 2000. (CMC and The Republican newspaper)

Arctic Dreams
Difficulty: Grade 6
Duration: 27:00
Published 1991 by Carl Fisher (rental)

Arctic Dreams was commissioned by James Keene for the 100th anniversary of the University of Illinois Symphonic and Concert Bands, and premiered by the University of Illinois Symphonic Band on January 26, 1991 with Mr. Keene conducting. The seven movements move forward without pause: *Inuit Landscape - Throat Singing with Laughter - Whispering Voices - Polar Night - Spring Light - The Hunt - Drum Dancer.*

In the words of the composer: "*Arctic Dreams* is a tone poem for symphonic wind ensemble, inspired by the Arctic and by the lives and legends of the Inuit (the 'Eskimos') who live there. I lived for a short time with an Inuit family in Pangnirtung, Baffin Island, just north of the Arctic Circle, and I was fascinated by their way of life, their humor, and their sense of mystery and wonder at the awesome nature around them. To me, the Arctic is like a great unconscious. Therefore, the title of Barry Lopez's wonderful book 'Arctic Dreams' seemed also an apt description of this music."

After a trombone solo suggesting the vastness of the Arctic landscape, Colgrass presents a series of tone images depicting throat singing and the majesty of the aurora borealis. Two movements, *Throat Singing with Laughter* and *Polar Night,* have vocal parts for band members to sing, although involving choir can be very effective. Colgrass employs many improvisational techniques to achieve each movement, and all players are stretched technically and musically. (Denise Grant)

Bali
Difficulty: Grade 4
Duration: 8:35
Published 2006 by Carl Fischer

Bali was commissioned by the Bishop Ireton High School Wind ensemble of Alexandria, Virginia, and is dedicated to that ensemble and its director, Randy Eyles. The work was inspired by music the composer encountered during two summers spent in Ubud, a small, artistic community in mountainous central Bali, and is based around the gamelan, a highly percussive ensemble found in Indonesia. In *Bali*, the composer strives to depict the "indomitable spirit" of the Balinese people, and does so not through the use of traditional folk melodies or nationalistic themes, but through use of symbolic sounds and infectious rhythms.

Written for a wind ensemble of 42 players, the three-section work includes parts for prepared piano and six percussionists who perform on standard percussion equipment plus fifteen bowls of various sizes and timbres: five ceramic bowls, five aluminum bowls, and five clay pots. The opening and closing movements are in 2/4 and marked at quarter note = 126. The middle section begins with a sudden and powerful explosion, a sound representing the tragic 2002 terrorist bombing in the capital city of Denpassar. It then moves quickly into a reflective period of mourning, focusing on three offstage oboes that symbolize a grieving Muslim community. This section stands in stark contrast to the outer two, requiring legato technique and muted brass. The work as a whole provides the opportunity to foster greater knowledge of diverse instrumental groupings and colors. (Teaching Music Through Performance in Band, Vol. 6. © GIA Publications, used by permission.)

Old Churches
Difficulty: Grade 2
Duration: 5:30
Commissioned and Published 2002 by the American Composers Forum
   (www.composersforum.org)
Published 2002 by BandQuest

The American Composers Forum helps composers engage with communities in groundbreaking composer residencies, designed to engage communities in the creative process and broaden the contexts in which new music is written, performed and heard. It means innovative approaches to teaching music while nurturing the next generation of composers, performers and audiences.

Michael Colgrass's goal in this Forum was to create music that was interesting, expressive and challenging, yet playable by students in the early stages of performing on their instruments and who are also unfamiliar with modern music techniques. His solution was to write a work based on Gregorian vocal chant with unison melodies. *Old Churches* uses Gregorian chant and graphic notation to create a slightly mysterious monastery scene filled with the prayers and chanting of monks in an old church. The chant unfolds through call and response patterns. One monk intones a musical idea, then the rest of the monks respond by singing back. This musical conversation continues throughout the piece, with the exception of a few brief interruptions. (CMC and The American Composers Forum)

Winds of Nagual: a musical fable for wind ensemble on the writings of Carlos Castaneda
Difficulty: Grade 6
Duration: 25:00.
Published 1987 by Carl Fischer

The *Winds of Nagual* is based on the writings of Carlos Castaneda about his 14-year apprenticeship with Juan Mattise, a Yaqui Indian sorcerer from northwestern Mexico. Castaneda met Don Juan while researching hallucinogenic plants for his master's thesis in anthropology at UCLA. Juan becomes Castaneda's mentor and trains him in Pre-Columbian techniques of sorcery, the overall purpose of which is to find the creative self—what Juan calls the "Nagual."

Each of the characters has a musical theme: Juan's is dark and ominous, yet gentle and kind; Carlos's is open, direct, and naïve. We hear Carlos's theme throughout the piece from constantly changing perspectives, as Juan submits him to long desert marches, encounters with terrifying powers, and altered states of reality. A comic aspect is added to the piece by Don Genaro, a sorcerer friend of Juan's who frightens Carlos with fantastic tricks, such as disappearing and reappearing at will.

The score is laced with programmatic indications such as "Juan entrances Carlos with a stare," "A horrible creature leaps at Carlos," "He feels a deep calm and joy," etc. The listener need not have read Castaneda's books to enjoy the work, and the composer doesn't expect anyone to follow an exact scenario. His objective is to capture the mood and atmosphere created by the books and to convey a feeling of the relationship that develops as a man of ancient wisdom tries to develop heart in an analytical young man of the technological age.

Movements include *The desert – Carlos meets Don Juan – Don Genaro satirizes Carlos – Carlos stares at the water and becomes a bubble – The gait of power – Asking twilight for calmness and power – Juan clowns for Carlos – Last conversation and farewell.*

Winds of Nagual was commissioned by the New England Conservatory Wind Ensemble with assistance of Massachusetts Council on the Arts. Its première was given on February 14, 1985 at Jordon Hall in Boston by the New England Conservatory Wind Ensemble, Frank Battisti, conductor. (CMC, The Database of Recorded American Music, and the composer's notes)

Douglas Court (b. 1963)

Douglas Court is a native of Toronto, Ontario and received his early musical training in The Salvation Army. He received his formal training at the University of Toronto, where he studied trumpet and graduated with a Bachelor of Music Education degree. He also studied composition at the University of South Florida.

While living in Toronto, Court worked as a freelance trumpet player performing with groups such as the Canadian Opera Company orchestra. From 1986 through 1995 he held the position of Divisional Music Director for The Salvation Army in the state of Florida. This position allowed for extensive work with young musicians, running summer music conservatories, teaching private lessons as well as conducting both adult and youth ensembles. Many of his instrumental and vocal pieces are published by The Salvation Army, and he has written for Curnow Music since 1994. (Curnow Music Press and interview with the composer)

Celtic Dance
Difficulty: Grade 2
Duration: 2:40
Published 1979 by Curnow Music Press

Celtic Dance was written for the 20th anniversary of the Vienna Band Camp in Vienna, Virginia. It is based on the Irish folk tune, *The Galway Piper,* and features the unmistakable flavor of Irish folk music and Irish dance, including foot stomping and a snare drum solo. The instrumentation includes double reeds, mallet percussion, timpani, and unpitched percussion, making this an interesting and fun work for young band. (Jeff Reynolds and interview with the composer)

Cityscapes
Difficulty: Grade 3
Duration: 4:50
Published 1999 by Curnow Music Press

Cityscapes was written for the Havergal College Symphonic Band and premiered at the Ford Centre for the Performing Arts in Toronto, Feb. 5 1998. Havergal College is a school for girls with a rich tradition located in the city of Toronto, Ontario. The college believes that a broad based education is vital to prepare a young woman to take her place in society, and seeks to instill each of its students a sense of her own worth as well as responsibility for developing her talents to the fullest. The landscape of the college, like the city of Toronto, continues to grow and has gone through many changes throughout the years.

The music of *Cityscapes* seeks to portray this growth beginning with a plaintive melody that begins to grow and evolve with the energy of new ideas. Throughout this process a sense of mission and determination begins to appear in the music. (© Curnow Music Press, used by permission)

Journey to a New World
Difficulty: Grade 2
Duration: 2:15
Published 2001 by Curnow Music Press

One of Canada's early "founding fathers" was French explorer Jacques Cartier, who set sail in 1534 on a voyage of discovery from the Normandy port of St. Malo. *Journey to a New World* mixes a lively contrapuntal style with the folk song, *A St. Malo, Beau Port de Mer*, which makes its appearance in the last half of the piece. This is also an excellent work through which to introduce young players to syncopation. (Fraser Linklater and Curnow Music Press, used by permission)

A recording of this work is available on the CD "North Winds—Canadian Wind Band Music," which may be ordered from the University of Manitoba, Faculty of Music, 65 Dafoe Road, Winnipeg, Manitoba, Canada R3T 2N2 or by calling (204) 474-9310.

Kawartha Legend
Difficulty: Grade 2
Duration: 2:20
Published 2003 by Curnow Music Press

The Kawartha Lakes are a series of clean, sparkling lakes and rivers located in Ontario two hours northeast of Toronto. Generations of Canadians have embraced this beautiful landscape and built cottages all over this region. Long before this, however, the area was home to the First Nations people of Canada. The name "Kawartha" given by the First Nations people actually means "Land of Shining Waters." The area is full of North American legends as the native people built their lives around this picturesque setting. The history and influence of the First Nations people are still visible today. This music seeks to describe the energy of the early settlers as well as the natural beauty of the landscape. (© Curnow Music Press, used by permission)

Land of the Silver Birch
Difficulty: Grade 1
Duration: 2:00
Published 1998 by Curnow Music Press

Land of the Silver Birch is a traditional Canadian folk song. The song's origins are unclear, although it may be of native origin, and dates from at least the

1930's. It is popular in the Boy Scouts and Girl Guides movements, and has been sung in Canadian schools and summer camps for years because of its evocation of the native peoples of North America. As is often the case with folk songs, nature is the subject matter. The words of the song express the writer's love for his homeland and the beauty of the Canadian landscape. The haunting, mysterious quality of the melody from the Huron First Nations people is one of its most engaging features. (Interview with the composer and Curnow Music Press, used by permission)

True North
Difficulty: Grade 2
Duration: 2:40
Published 1997 by Curnow Music Press

This folk song fantasy uses two well-known Canadian folk songs. *Vive la Canadienne* was originally an old French tune that was borrowed by a French-Canadian songwriter in praise of the Canadian girl. *Let Me Fish off Cape St. Mary* is one of many beautiful Newfoundland folk songs displaying the love and devotion Newfoundlanders have for their home province. This piece also contains fragments of *The Maple Leaf Forever*, a song portraying the symbol which, having been associated with this great country, is displayed on the Canadian flag. (© Curnow Music Press, used by permission)

Wedgewood Festival
Difficulty: Grade 1
Duration: 2:10
Published 1996 by Curnow Music Press

This piece is named for the school at which the composer first experienced music in the public school system in Canada. It was composed as a tribute to the belief that a positive start in music can give students years of enjoyment and a great appreciation of their art. (© Curnow Music Press, used by permission)

CLIFFORD CRAWLEY (B. 1929)

CLIFFORD CRAWLEY WAS BORN and educated in England. He holds degrees from the University of Durham and diplomas from the Royal College of Music and Trinity College, London. He also studied briefly with composers Lennox Berkeley and Humphrey Searle. Before coming to Canada he taught in both elementary and secondary schools and was involved in teacher training as Head of Music in a College of Education.

Affiliated with the Canadian League of Composers and the Canadian Music Centre, he has over eighty published compositions, including a number in festival and conservatory lists. His musical style has been described as "warmly human," "contemporary [but] accessible and eclectic" (Encyclopedia of Music in Canada 1992: 328). Eclecticism is consistent with his belief that "originality is not necessarily something new but often [the result of] looking at the familiar in a different way."

He is Professor Emeritus at Queen's University, having taught composition and music education there from 1973 to 1993. He has worked as a music consultant in Central America and Asia, and participated in many Composer/Artist in the Classroom programs. After ten years in Toronto, he now lives and enjoys an active musical life in St. John's, Newfoundland. (CMC and The Canadian Encyclopedia)

Canadian Heritage: overture for concert band based on traditional airs and themes by Dunbar Moodie (1797–1869) and students of Centennial High School, Belleville, Ontario
Difficulty: Grade 3
Duration: 6:00
Composed in 1986
Available through CMC (www.musiccentre.ca)

Canadian Heritage was written as part of a "Composer in the Classroom" project funded by the Ontario Arts Council. It includes a tune discovered by the Canadian composer Gena Branscombe (1881–1977) who was born near Belleville, Ontario, close to Centennial High School where the project took place. Other tunes included in the work were written by members of the high school band, with the composer working in conjunction with the students. *Canadian Heritage* is in the key of F throughout, and the names of the participating students are included in the score. (Interview with the composer)

May-Day
Difficulty: Grade 5
Duration: 7:30
Composed in 1978
Available through CMC (www.musiccentre.ca)

Written for the wind ensemble of Queen's University in Kingston, Ontario, *May-Day* was premiered by that ensemble in 1978 with Duane Bates conducting. It is written in a 12-note idiom—not strictly as used by Schoenberg, but definitely not tonal. Allegro, Alla Marcia, Andante sostenuto, Allegretto, and Adagio sections depict the title in styles ranging from medieval festivities to emergencies on the high seas. (Interview with the composer)

Tyendinaga: Legend for concert band
Difficulty: Grade 4
Duration: 8:00
Composed in 1978
Available through CMC (www.musiccentre.ca)

Tyendinaga is Clifford Crawley's rhapsodic elaboration of an Iroquois Indian Lullaby. It was commissioned by the Napanee Secondary School Music Department, and the title directly relates to the Indian reservation south of Napanee. The lullaby, *Ho Ho Watanay,* roughly translates to "Sleep, little one." Although based on an Iroquois melody, the piece does not sound aboriginal.

The melody is quoted in solo flute and solo clarinet at the beginning and then developed and transformed as the work progresses. Variation one is in a fast tempo with simple meter changes, and uses a version of the theme altered rhythmically to incorporate syncopation. The second variation is slow and lyrical, with a new melody generated from the notes of the theme. This new melody is developed at considerable length, primarily thorough changes in orchestration. Variation three is fast, but heavy and warlike with a number of solo drum figures. Another new melody, a derivative of the syncopated melody in variation one, appears here. Also appearing are many meter changes that are often in complex relationship to each other. The fourth variation, another lyrical section, presents two new melodies: one derived from the melody in variation two, the other closely related to the theme but with octave displacements of some notes. Variation five opens with a fanfare, then recalls the unadorned theme and all of its variants from the entire composition. Dissonant counterpoint, rhythmic challenges, and rapid changes of style all result in a fascinating work with relentless forward energy. (CMC, Keith Kinder and interview with the composer)

A pedagogical discussion of this work can be found on page 48 of *Guidelist of Unpublished Canadian Band Music Suitable for Student Performers* by Patricia Martin Shand.

JIM DUFF (B. 1941)

JIM DUFF, A NATIVE of Newfoundland, holds a Diploma of Fine Arts from the University of Calgary, Alberta, a Bachelor of Music from Berklee College of Music, Boston, Massachusetts, and a Masters of Music from North Texas State University in Denton, Texas.

Besides his role as instrumental instructor and music coordinator with Newfoundland's Eastern School District, Mr. Duff has acted as instructor in trombone, Jazz Ensemble, Jazz Band Arranging, North American Popular Music, and Instrumental Teaching Methods at Memorial University of Newfoundland. Other musical activities include conducting and adjudicating both locally and nationally, and clinics in arranging and concert and jazz band technique. He has served for many years as musical director, performer, composer and arranger, and sound consultant for many CBC radio and television series and specials, and has acted as leader of his own big band for concerts and numerous other occasions. For the past twelve years he has worked closely with the Newfoundland Symphony Orchestra as composer, arranger, and conductor for their annual Gala and Pops concerts.

Mr. Duff has been awarded numerous commissions, including those from the Newfoundland Symphony Orchestra, the Atlantic Arts Trio, the Memorial University String Quartet, Kenneth Knowles, the Avalon East District Honours Band, the Arnprior District High School Band (Ontario), the Henry Gordon Academy (Labrador), the Newfoundland Symphony Youth Choir, the Memorial University Concert Choir, Canada Winter Games (opening ceremonies), the Newfoundland government/CBC (Soiree '99), Cabot 500th Anniversary, and CBC national radio (Sunrise Celebration). His compositions and arrangements have been performed by symphony orchestras and concert bands in both Canada and the United States, and his concert band compositions and arrangements have been published and distributed worldwide by Alfred Publishing Company and Warner/Chappell Music, Inc. (Jim Duff)

Cape St. Mary's
Difficulty: Grade 2
Duration: 2:44
Published 1986 by Columbia Pictures/Belwin

This work is an arrangement of a folk song that is one of the all-time favorites of Newfoundland. Young bands should perform it in legato style throughout except for clearly defined staccatos at the beginning and end. Careful attention to dynamics and phrasing will ensure a successful performance. (Jim Duff)

Galactic March
Difficulty: Grade 3
Duration: 2:20
Published 1991 by Columbia Pictures/Belwin

This piece is reminiscent of today's many popular space themes. Triplets should be carefully articulated, and accents should contrast with non-accented notes. The players will learn to make clear distinctions between the marcato A and legato B sections, with tenuto and staccato articulations clearly defined. (Jim Duff)

Greenwood Overture
Difficulty: Grade 2
Duration 4:13
Published 1992 by Alfred Publishing

An inspiring composition in ABA form, *Greenwood Overture* begins with a glorious fanfare that richly introduces a lively Allegro section. The primary theme, stated by the trumpets and repeated by the woodwinds, is supported by syncopated harmonies in the low brass and reinforced by the percussion. A slow, sparkling B section offers both soli and tutti passages for contrast and leads to a recapitulation of the original theme. (© Alfred Publishing Co., Inc., used by permission)

March and Interlude
Difficulty: Grade 2
Duration 3:40
Published 1990 by Alfred Publishing

This composition was commissioned by the Eastern Music Camp, Mount Pearl, Newfoundland, through a grant from the Newfoundland and Labrador Arts Council, and is an excellent work for young band. Care should be taken to maintain a steady tempo throughout the march with attention to precise and balanced low-brass rhythmic accompaniment. The interlude should be played in a flowing style with all notes receiving full value. Attention to balance (particularly between countermelodies and melody), articulation, and dynamics will lead to a successful performance. (Jim Duff)

Newfoundland Folk Song
Difficulty: Grade 3
Duration: 3:30
Published 1989 by Alfred Publishing

This sensitive arrangement by Jim Duff is based on the lovely folk song *She's Like the Swallow,* one of the most beautiful of all Newfoundland folk songs, and a favorite of composers writing in many genres. It features an alto saxophone solo and beautiful scoring that creates a warm wash of color to support the reflective melody. For his easy arrangement of this exquisite song of unrequited love, Duff chose one of the simpler versions, a straightforward Dorian melody. While the melody is presented unadorned throughout, the accompaniment incorporates chromatically inflected harmony, several countermelodies and textural devices such as harmonic pyramids that are perhaps inspired by Grainger's idea of "accompaniment variation." A hint of arch form provides a satisfying sense of musical resolution. (Keith Kinder and Alfred Publishing Co., Inc., used by permission)

A recording of this work is available on the CD "North Winds—Canadian Wind Band Music," which may be ordered from the University of Manitoba, Faculty of Music, 65 Dafoe Road, Winnipeg, Manitoba, Canada R3T 2N2 or by calling (204) 474-9310.

Petty Harbour Bait Skiff
Difficulty: Grade 3
Duration: 3:30
Published 1994 by Alfred Publishing

Jim Duff arranged this popular folk song in recognition of Newfoundland's primary resource – fishing. The bait skiff is a small boat used for catching fish bait. Petty Harbour is a fishing village a short distance from St. John's, the province's capital city. The song came about as the result of a tragedy. On June 8, 1852, a bait skiff (or trap skiff—26 to 32 feet long) was caught in a squall near Petty Harbour while returning from Conception Bay. Everyone in the community witnessed the event but all were powerless to help the men. They drowned one by one, except a boy clinging to the mast. Jacob Chafe successfully rescued the boy. The famous Newfoundland folk song, *The Petty Harbour Bait Skiff* recalls the event. It was composed soon after the tragedy by John Grace of St. John's, where there was "crying and lamenting in the streets" on learning of the fate of Skipper John French and his crew "all on the eighth of June." Only one of the crew, "young Menshon," was saved by "Jacob Chafe, that hero brave." Edward Chafe said that when he was little his grandfather had a copper sundial in the parlor that was presented to Jacob Chafe, the Hero Brave, in recognition of his courage and selflessness. The work opens with a euphonium solo that is a substantial challenge for players at this level. Chromatic harmony presents tuning challenges. (Keith Kinder and Alfred Publishing Co., Inc., used by permission)

A recording of this work is available on the CD "North Winds—Canadian Wind Band Music," which may be ordered from the University of Manitoba, Faculty of Music, 65 Dafoe Road, Winnipeg, Manitoba, Canada R3T 2N2 or by calling (204) 474-9310. A recording of this work also is available on the CD "A Lakeshore Concert," by the Lakeshore Concert Band of Montreal, and may be ordered by emailing the band at *lakeshoreconcertband@coolgoose.com.*

A Seaside Ballad
Difficulty: Grade 3
Duration: 4:00
Published 1991 by Alfred Publishing

This ballad in ABA form provides an opportunity to display expression and phrasing in the cantabile style. Following the mood-setting introduction, the themes are passed between various sections of the band and supported by sustained harmonic accompaniment and countermelodies. Careful attention should be given to overall balance, especially where countermelodies are introduced. (Jim Duff)

Terra Nova Overture
Difficulty: Grade 3
Duration: 4:30
Published 1991 by Alfred Publishing

Following a majestic opening, a short fanfare introduces the themes of the first section of this piece in ABA form. Ample opportunity is provided for featuring various sections of the band, and the contrasting moods will add interest to both performers and listeners alike. Care should be taken to maintain a steady tempo in the A section with precise accompaniment by the low brass. The players must ensure that countermelodies in the B section are balanced with the melody, and that attention is given to the expression marks provided. (Jim Duff)

BRENT DUTTON (B. 1950)

BRENT DUTTON, PROFESSOR OF music at San Diego State University, is a musician of diverse interests and pursuits. He has an amalgam of careers as composer, performer, teacher, arranger and conductor. His musical studies began at age nine in his native Canada. He began composing at age ten and attended the Royal Conservatory of Music while still in high school. He holds master's and doctoral degrees from the Oberlin Conservatory of Music.

Prior to his appointment at San Diego State Mr. Dutton served on the music faculties of the Oberlin Conservatory of Music, the California Institute of the Arts and Central Michigan University. He was also the brass coach for the Jeunesses Musicales World Orchestra from 1986–92 in Poland, Germany, Sweden, Norway, Finland, The Soviet Union, Uruguay, Argentina, Canada and Denmark.

He has received over 30 awards for his work including two Yaddo Fellowships, five Canada Council Arts Bursaries, The Phi Kappa Lambda Excellence Award (Oberlin) and the Royal Conservatory Of Music Silver Medal for Excellence. He has three times (1987,1989, 1993) been named Outstanding Professor of the Year for Music at San Diego State University and in 1985 was named Distinguished Professor of the Year for his College. He was the Phi Beta Kappa Lecturer for SDSU in the spring of 1993, the same year that he was elected to the Canadian Music Centre as Associate Composer.

Prof. Dutton's compositions embrace a wide field of interests and techniques. The overriding compositional principle in this varied approach is a keen interest in balancing the emotive and structural aspects of the music so that both are mutually satisfying.

As a performer, he has played as a soloist, chamber musician and orchestral musician on the tuba throughout the world. He has been a member of the Cleveland Orchestra, L'Orchestre Symphonique du Québec, Grand Ballet Canadien, Jeunesses Musicales World Orchestra, the San Diego Symphony, The San Diego Brass Consort and Westwind Brass, as well as many other professional ensembles. He was the first tubist to do a recital tour of Canada. (CMC and interview with the composer)

Patrician Dances
Difficulty: grade 6
Duration: 22:00
Composed in 1995
Available through CMC (www.musiccentre.ca)

The composer writes: *Patrician Dances* are neither patrician nor are they dances, and yet they are both. Nothing is what it seems to be and yet it is. The work is to be played without break, and should appear in the concert program in this fashion:

Movements: *I. Lavolta - Vamp I - II. Syncretic Padam (slow waltz) - Vamp II - III. Ghost Tangos - Vamp III - IV. A Scurry (Trenchmore/trepak).* (CMC)

Symphony No. 5: Dark Spirals
Difficulty: grade 6
Duration: 40:00
Composed in 1984
Available through CMC (www.musiccentre.ca)

The four movements of this work are titled: *I. Lame - II. Lament - III. Scherzo Fou - IV. Endings.* The composer dedicates it: "For those I have loved and lost. In memory of my father."

The composer writes: Through the course of a life some people are fortunate enough to have relationships with a few other people that are very deep and intense. The most profound of these relationships can take on a magical quality that gives added meaning to life. The world can see the outside of the shell/relationship and know that it is beautiful, but only the two people in the relationship can know the inside of the shell and its secrets. My father was very important to me and we had a very special bond. When he died I was very disturbed and found my loss difficult to deal with. Words did not seem to help me. I finally decided to put my feelings into a composition that would tell of my pain of loss and remembrance of joy. (CMC)

Malcolm Forsyth (b. 1936)

Malcolm Forsyth, honored as Canadian Composer of the Year in 1989, has earned international recognition as one of Canada's leading composers. Born in 1936 in Pietermaritzburg, South Africa, Forsyth majored in trombone, conducting and composition at the University of Cape Town and played trombone 8 years with the Cape Town Symphony Orchestra (CTSO) while obtaining his Master's and subsequently Doctorate degrees. His career as a composer was launched in 1962 when the CTSO performed *Overture Erewhon,* and its success led to an invitation to write the *Jubilee Overture* for the orchestra's 50th anniversary in 1964.

In 1968, Forsyth emigrated to Canada and settled in Edmonton, where he joined the Edmonton Symphony Orchestra, playing first bass trombone and then, for the next eight years, playing as principal. He also joined the faculty at the University of Alberta, teaching theory, composition and conducting. Forsyth retired from the faculty in 2002, after serving as the University's composer-in-residence.

Sketches from Natal, commissioned and broadcast by the Canadian Broadcasting Corporation in 1970, was Forsyth's première contribution to Canadian music. This vibrant work for chamber orchestra was the first of many subsequent compositions that explore the tribal rhythms of his native country. Other works Forsyth produced during the seventies include the critically acclaimed *Concerto for Piano and Orchestra* (1979), two symphonies, several works for brass and woodwind ensemble, as well as two concerti grossi written for the Canadian Brass.

During the 1980's, following a year of study in London, England, Forsyth was inspired to compose numerous symphonic and chamber works. From this period, two orchestral compositions in particular embody his unique style: *African Ode* (Symphony No. 3) (1981) depicts the stark contrasts and rhythmic vitality of his native land, and *Atayoskewin* (Suite for Orchestra), a powerful portrayal of Canada's North, was hailed as "a masterpiece" at its premiere in 1984, and in 1987 it won the first JUNO for Best Classical Composition.

During the 1990's he composed such acclaimed works as *Electra Rising: Concerto for Violoncello and Orchestra,* written for his daughter Amanda, and *Evangeline.* The latter, based on the poem by Henry Longfellow, tells the fictional account of the historic voyage of the Acadians expelled from Nova Scotia in 1755. He has gone on to win two more JUNO awards for Best Classical Composition (more than anyone else), in 1995 for *Sketches from Natal,* and in 1998 for *Electra Rising.* His *Double Concerto* for viola, cello and orchestra, was premiered in 2004 by the Edmonton Symphony Orchestra, and his work has been extensively recorded. (CMC)

Colour Wheel
Difficulty: Grade 5
Duration: ca. 7:00
Published 1978 by Counterpoint Musical Services (www.counterpointmusic.ca)

Forsyth's varied output as one of Canada's most prolific and often-performed composers includes *Colour Wheel* for wind band. *Colour Wheel* was commissioned by the Alberta Chapter of the Canadian Band Directors' Association, and premiered at the 1977 convention of the Association with the composer conducting the Alberta Honor Band.

The composer has indicated that in choosing a visual art title, he intended to invoke both an artist's circular palette of pure colors and a circular painting designed so that it appears to spin when viewed. The work is rather dark in quality, thickly scored, with layered independent textures that exploit the winds in combination with abundant percussion.

The first section is slow and consists of heavy quintal and polytonal harmonies, perhaps denoting the unmixed colors of the artist's pallet. The second section is much faster and marked "with strong rhythm and spirit-like" by the composer, perhaps reflecting the sweeping lines and blending of colors by a painter in action. The melodic material is based on short motivic fragments that are developed and expanded in an A-B-A-B-A form, with the last A section marked "more brilliant" – perhaps a finished painting. Forsyth saves a major chord for the final statement. (CMC, Keith Kinder, and Michael Purves-Smith)

Kaleidoscope
Difficulty: Grade 6
Duration: 5:00
Published 1989 by Counterpoint Musical Services (www.counterpointmusic.ca)

The Alberta Band Association commissioned this work for the Senior Wind Ensemble of Alberta College for performance at the Alberta Music Convention in 1989. It received its premiere at the Edmonton Convention Center under the direction of Dennis Prime. The title reflects the composer's continuing fascination for the large palette of instrumental color in the concert band.

Cast in a loose rondo form, three sections are alternated in brilliant scoring. The first is a rhythmic, fanfare-like theme, where the subtle alternation of regular with triplet eighth notes provides a scintillating texture built upon two formations of the octatonic scale in mirror inversion. The second is a faster, dance-like pattern with the woodwinds leading, interjected by stabs of color from muted brass and percussion. A third idea, marked "with humor," has the cornets dancing in a pattern of fast, repeated notes. The final statement of the first theme ushers in a brilliant closing idea in the brass, which brings the piece to its dazzling conclusion. (Interview with the composer)

HARRY FREEDMAN (1922–2005)

HARRY FREEDMAN WAS BORN in Poland and came to Canada with his family when he was three. His early training was as a visual artist but during his teens he developed an interest in jazz that soon spread to classical music. At eighteen, he made the break and began studying clarinet. After four years in the RCAF during the war, he came to Toronto to study oboe with Perry Bauman and composition with John Weinzweig at the Royal Conservatory of Music. The following year he joined the Toronto Symphony Orchestra as its English horn player, a post he held for 24 years until he resigned in 1970 to compose full time. Apart from brief periods with Aaron Copland and Olivier Messiaen at Tanglewood in 1949) and Ernst Krenek in Toronto in 1953, the 5 years he spent with Weinzweig were the extent of his formal studies in composition.

Freedman is one of Canada's most frequently performed composers. His output has given the music world a vast array of over 200 compositions ranging from solo voice to choir, from full orchestral symphonies to string, wind and brass ensembles, from theater to dance stage and from film to television programs.

Of the many honors his music has garnered, two stood out in Freedman's mind. In 1970, the Brian Macdonald ballet *5 OVER 13*, for which Freedman wrote the music, received front-page headlines when the Royal Winnipeg Ballet performed it in Rotterdam. And in 1988, *Borealis*, for orchestra and four choirs, was presented in Paris at the International Rostrum of Composers, an annual symposium of music producers (radio) who present broadcast recordings of the most interesting pieces they have heard during the past year. Sixty compositions from 32 countries were presented. *Borealis* placed 4th—which, as Freedman points out, was the musical equivalent of being nominated for the Booker Prize. As a result of this recognition, *Borealis* was performed twenty-two times all over the world.

He was a founding member of the Canadian League of Composers (president, 1975–78) and of the Guild of Canadian Film Composers. In 1967, he was chosen to represent Canada at the 2nd Festival of Music of the Americas and Spain in Madrid, where his *First Symphony* was performed. In 1970 he won the Etrog (now called the Genie) for best music in a feature film at the Canadian Film Awards. In 1984 he was appointed an Officer of the Order of Canada in recognition of the craftsmanship of his works, his contribution to Canadian musical life as a performer with the Toronto Symphony Orchestra, his services to music organizations, and his work as an educator. (CMC)

A la Claire Fontaine
Difficulty: Grade 2
Duration: 3:45
Composed in 1970
Available through CMC (www.musiccentre.ca)

A wind player himself, Harry Freedman was always interested in the education of young wind performers. In the early 1970's he was involved in a "Composer in the Classroom" project in the Toronto schools, and during that time produced this arrangement of the Québec folk song, *A la Claire Fontaine,* especially for middle school bands. The work focuses on the lyrical side of band performance, and, since Freedman believed that every player should have an interesting part, is transparently scored and full of contrapuntal textures. This song is among the best known and oldest of all Canadian folk songs, and dates back to the earliest French settlements in Nova Scotia.

Freedman's setting is remarkable in many ways. Quiet dynamics are prevalent, some marked "as soft as possible." It is tonally grounded in E-flat, but the accompaniment is built from a series of harmonic seconds, rendering it essentially atonal. Since the melody is presented very simply and the percussionists are asked to improvise quietly, performance requires careful listening by all players. The resulting soundscape is highly colored and is some of the gentlest music written for band. (CMC and Keith Kinder)

A recording of this work is available on the CD "North Winds—Canadian Wind Band Music," which may be ordered from the University of Manitoba, Faculty of Music, 65 Dafoe Road, Winnipeg, Manitoba, Canada R3T 2N2 or by calling (204) 474-9310.

Laurentian Moods
Difficulty: Grade 4
Duration: 7:00
Composed in 1961
Available through CMC (www.musiccentre.ca)

This accomplished composer's *Laurentian Moods* is an early work commissioned by the band at Barrie Collegiate High School in Barrie, Ontario for their performance at the 1962 World's Fair in Seattle, Washington. As the title suggests (the Laurentians are a mountain range north of Montreal) the melodies are French-Canadian folk songs from Québec.

While all sections are bridged, this work is closer to a suite than a medley. Each tune is developed to a much greater degree than in a medley. The scoring is very transparent and the harmony is imaginative with polychords, quintal and quartal sonorities, and complex chords created by the contrapuntal movement of voices. Each of the four tunes is subjected to substantial development in highly creative ways. For example, the tune *La-bas, sur les Montagnes* is presented initially as a canon at the fifth, then unison in the low voices accompanied only by a three-voice chromatic chorale played by trumpets with harmon mutes – a texture that even today sounds startlingly innovative. This is an outstanding work that remains little known. The transparent scoring may have intimidated band directors who were used to thicker textures, but today this is no longer a reason to ignore such a composition. (CMC and Keith Kinder)

Sonata for Wind Orchestra
Difficulty: Grade 6
Duration: 18:00
Composed in 1990
Available through CMC (www.musiccentre.ca)

This tone poem was written for the Toronto Symphony Youth Orchestra's winds, brass, and percussion, and is technically challenging. Focusing largely on line, it presents chromatic counterpoint at fast tempos with rapidly shifting meter. Scored to feature primarily the softer sonorities of the three sections, it also has some startling dynamics for contrast. A brisk opening featuring mixed meter is followed by constantly changing texture, orchestral pyramids, and sound clouds. Long crescendos and diminuendos require excellent control. Demanding and energetic, *Sonata for Wind Orchestra* is a noteworthy addition to the wind band repertoire. (CMC and Keith Kinder)

VINCE GASSI (B. 1959)

VINCE GASSI IS A graduate of the University of Western Ontario Faculty of Music in London, Ontario. He studied composing and arranging at the Dick Grove School of Music in Los Angeles, California. While attending this school he also studied trumpet with the late Dr. Claude Gordon. Mr. Gassi has written works for concert band, orchestra, jazz ensemble, woodwind and brass quintets and choirs; and recently scored a television commercial and a short film. In addition to performing and composing, Mr. Gassi has taught in both elementary and secondary schools and is currently teaching instrumental music at Mary Ward Catholic Secondary School in Toronto, Ontario. (Interview with the composer and Eighth Note Publications, used by permission)

Ships With Sails Unfurled
Difficulty: Grade 3
Duration: 4:20
Published 2004 by Eighth Note Publications (www.enpmusic.com)

This work describing the voyage of Columbus to the New World was written for a high school band in Toronto especially for their concert tour to Austria and Germany. In the early morning of August 3, 1492, Christopher Columbus went aboard the Santa Maria and gave the command to unfurl the sails. When the wind caught the sails, the three caravels were off and they had an uncharted ocean all to themselves. This programmatic work is in four movements: *Atlantic Crossing,* which captures the sense of adventure at the outset of such an epic journey; *First Contact,* which recalls the good will and free exchange of gifts and ideas, and the attempt to understand languages completely foreign to each side; *Caravels of Doom,* a somber mood describing the terrible effects of the disease that the Europeans brought with them; and *The Great Migration,* which recaps the opening theme, but this time it is not Columbus crossing the ocean but the hundreds of thousands of immigrants that embarked on the same bold adventure in the great migration of 1880–1920. Composing this piece was new territory for the composer as well, as it was his first serious piece for concert band. (Interview with the composer and Eighth Note Publications, used by permission)

James McDonald Gayfer (1916–1997)

Toronto native James Gayfer received his academic and musical education with Toronto Schools, the Royal Conservatory of Music (Toronto); the Royal Military School of Music (Kneller Hall), where he became a friend and associate of Ralph Vaughan Williams; the Royal College; and the Royal Academy of Music, London, England.

From 1942–67, he served in the Canadian Army Active and Regular Force in England, NW Europe, Germany, Korea and Japan. From 1935–42 he maintained an extensive journal describing his musical studies and thoughts. In 1953 he was appointed the first Director of Music of the Regimental Band of the Canadian Guards, and from 1961–66 the first Musical Training Officer of the new Canadian Forces School of Music at Esquimalt, B.C. Here he formed and directed a chamber choir, produced and directed opera and musical theatre, as well as conducted band and orchestral concerts. Upon retiring from the Army in 1967, he initiated and taught an instrumental music program in Ontario at Southwood Secondary School, Cambridge and Champlain High School, Pembroke.

From 1972, his many posts included Associate Professor of Instrumental Music Education at Dalhousie University, Halifax, founder-director of the Petawawa Legion (517) Community Band and Band School, and organist-choir director at St. George's Chapel, CFB Petawawa. He also resumed the direction of the Pembroke Community Choir. Gayfer continued his career as teacher-director of the Lindsay Kinsmen Band from 1980–83. In 1983 he was awarded the Order of St. John (Serving Brother) for *St. John Ambulance Canadian Centennial March* and was honored more recently by the Canadian Band Association for his prize-winning march *On Parliament Hill* and his *Fanfare, Toccata and March*.

"I am a traditional composer: non-serial, non-aleatoric or electronic," Gayfer said. "However, I do see great value and significance in all forms of creative expression, as long as it contains real ideas and concepts, in order to communicate, first for the composer, then for the performer and then for the listener. Give me a 'tune,' and I'll follow you anywhere!" (CMC, The Canadian Encyclopedia, and E. F. Lloyd Hiscock)

Canadian Landscape
Difficulty: Grade 3
Duration: 6:00
Published 1974 by Boosey & Hawkes (rental)

Canadian Landscape began as a film score, and was transcribed for orchestra before being expanded and rescored for band in 1974. The composer wrote, "The piece is intended to describe, in montage or kaleidoscope fashion, the feelings aroused by the varied aspects and scenery of our vast country from coast to coast."

The contrasting and highly descriptive montages include seven movements. *The Rolling Countryside* is portrayed with a gently undulating theme in the horns marked andante pastorale, while *Farmlands, Towns and Villages* has a light flute melody reminiscent of Gershwin's street music from *An American in Paris*. *Reflections in Forest Solitude* is lightly scored and introspective in its simplicity. A brief recitative introduces *Headlands*. A fanfare-like flourish creates a feeling of the sea crashing on the rocks, leading to a lento misterioso section entitled *Prairie and Sea-Coast Vistas*. Clarinets and flutes portray the table-flat prairie in parallel fourths while the unison melody underneath in the bass rises and falls over a contrasting range of two octaves, conjuring images of the swell of the sea. The lines become chromatic and more intense and mysterious, finally dying away. *The Broad Land* again presents the opening themes, but stronger and more densely scored, building up to *Great Trees and Mountains*. A mighty allargando brings the piece to a satisfying and thunderous end. (Denise Grant and E. F. Lloyd Hiscock)

A recording of this work is available on the CD "Concert in the Park," disk number SMCD5079, by the Edmonton Wind Ensemble, and may be ordered from the Canadian Music Centre (www.musiccentre.ca).

Royal Visit
Difficulty: Grade 4
Duration: 6:05
Published 1959 by Boosey & Hawkes

This stately grand ceremonial march reminiscent of Walton's *Crown Imperial* was composed for the October 1957 visit of Queen Elizabeth and Prince Philip to Canada. The fanfare opening contrasts with a more lyrical section in 3/4 and a stately trio. The march ends with a fanfare. Following the performance for Her Majesty, Gayfer was honored with a personal introduction. (CMC, E. F. Lloyd Hiscock, and Patricia Shand)

A pedagogical discussion of this work can be found on page 112 of *Canadian Music: A Selective Guidelist for Teachers* by Patricia Martin Shand.

The Wells of Marah: Episodes in the saga of the Selkirk settlers in Canada
Difficulty: Grade 4
Duration: 11:00
Composed in 1972
Available through CMC (www.musiccentre.ca)

Commissioned by the Barrie Central Collegiate Band of Barrie, Ontario, *The Wells of Marah* musically compares the exodus out of Egypt (Exodus 15:23) to episodes in the saga of the Selkirk settlers.

In the early 19th century, a large number of Scottish farmers had lost their farms in the fertile valley of the Red River to the Northwest Fur Company. Thomas Douglas, earl of Selkirk, became interested in relocating them to present-day Winnipeg. In 1812 the first group of Selkirk's settlers began to arrive from Hudson Bay, where they had spent the previous winter. Having been forced in mid-summer to leave the Red River district, many were bitter about resettling.

Marah is a Hebrew name meaning "bitterness." It was the name of a place the Israelites visited briefly after their Exodus from Egypt, after the Red Sea crossing. The composer of this work explains that the Selkirk settlers of Canada, like the Israelites, "...drank of the bitter wells of Marah before they found their Canaan in West Guillimbury Township below Barrie. "

The music certainly conveys feelings of suffering and hardship. Set in ABA form, it is an interesting study in contrasts and in tone painting, suggesting a film score. The link with Canadian history is also of interest. A quiet opening introduces a calm, lyrical main theme with meter changes of 4/4, 5/4, and 6/4. The A section features gradual increases in speed, dynamics, and intensity. The B section is marked molto calmato e diminuendo, and a D.S. leads back to the A section. The final crescendo in the coda is a natural resolution to the suffering, and conjures up visions and feelings of arriving in a promised land. (CMC, E. F. Lloyd Hiscock, and Patricia Shand)

A pedagogical discussion of this work can be found on page 55 of *Guidelist of Unpublished Canadian Band Music Suitable for Student Performers* by Patricia Martin Shand.

ALAN GILLILAND (B. 1965)

ALLAN GILLILAND WAS BORN in Darvel, Scotland and immigrated to Canada in 1972. He holds a diploma in Jazz Studies (trumpet) from Humber College, a Bachelor of music degree in performance and a Master of music degree in composition from the University of Alberta, where he studied with Violet Archer, Malcolm Forsyth and Howard Bashaw. He has written music for solo instruments, orchestra, choir, brass quintet, wind ensemble, big band, film, television and theatre. His music has been performed by many ensembles, including the Edmonton Symphony Orchestra, the Vancouver Symphony Orchestra, ProCoro Canada, the Canadian Brass, the Winnipeg Symphony Orchestra, the New York Pops, the International Symphony Orchestra, the Hammerhead Consort, the Brian Webb Dance Company, the Missoula Symphony Orchestra, the Tommy Banks Big Band, the Boston Pops, and the brass section of the New York Philharmonic.

For five years (1999–2004) he was Composer-in-Residence with the Edmonton Symphony Orchestra (ESO), writing 11 works for the ESO including concertos for oboe, trumpet, violin, 2 harps and clarinet. Other highlights include the *Winspear Fanfare* composed for the opening of the Winspear Centre, the *Concerto for Trumpet & Orchestra* premiered by Jens Lindemann and the ESO, *An Overture for the Worlds* commissioned for the opening ceremonies of the IAAF World Championships in Athletics, *Dreaming of the Masters I*, a jazz concerto written for clarinetist James Campbell and given its American premiere in 2004 by the Boston Pops, *Alberta Echoes,* a work for orchestra and dancers commissioned to celebrate Alberta's centennial and performed for Her Majesty Queen Elizabeth II and His Royal Highness The Duke of Edinburgh, and the musicals *The Seventh Circle* and *Dead Beats.* In 2002 his orchestral work *On the Shoulders of Giants* took first prize at the prestigious Winnipeg Symphony Orchestra's Centara New Music Festival Composers Competition.

Gilliland has also won composition contests sponsored by ProCoro Canada and the Alberta Band Association as well as first place in the Jean Coulthard Competition for Composers and the Lydia Pals Composers Competition. He is an Associate Composer with the Canadian Music Centre and a member of the Canadian League of Composers, and has taught at the University of Alberta and Red Deer College. As a trumpet player, he has been a regular member of the Tommy Banks Big Band and has lead his own jazz groups, most notably The Creative Opportunity Orchestra (CO2). He has also performed with the Edmonton Symphony Orchestra, Edmonton Opera and Capital Brass. He is now Head of the Composition major at Grant MacEwan College in Edmonton. (CMC)

Dreamscapes
Difficulty: Grade 3
Duration: 5:58
Composed 2003
Available from the composer (email gillilanda@macewan.ca)

Dreamscapes is written in a minimalist style and uses portions of a fanfare that the composer had previously written for a CBC program. *Dreamscapes* won an Alberta Band Association award for new wind band music in 2006. A slow mysterioso opening gives way to an alto saxophone solo in 3/4 time. Halfway through the work the texture and tempo change dramatically with a series of bell tones by both brass and woodwinds. The work concludes with a satisfying woodwind sweep to a major chord. (Fraser Linklater)

A recording of this work is available on the CD "North Winds—Canadian Wind Band Music," which may be ordered from the University of Manitoba, Faculty of Music, 65 Dafoe Road, Winnipeg, Manitoba, Canada R3T 2N2 or by calling (204) 474-9310.

DEREK HEALEY (B. 1936)

DEREK HEALEY WAS BORN in Wargrave, England and studied composition with Herbert Howells at the Royal College of Music in London, winning the Cobbett, Farrar and Sullivan Prizes. Later studies took Healey to Italy. In 1969 Healey moved to Canada where he received his doctorate from the University of Toronto and where he subsequently taught at the Universities of Victoria, Toronto and Guelph. Ten years later he immigrated to the United States to become Professor of Musical Composition at the University of Oregon at Eugene. After nine years on the West Coast he returned to England to become Academic Professor of Music at the RAF School of Music. Upon retiring he returned to North America, now residing in Brooklyn, New York. His ties with Canada are such that we may reasonably include him here: he received his doctorate from the University of Toronto; taught for many years at Canadian universities; and is still an associate composer of the Canadian Music Centre. Most important, many of his sources of inspiration are Canadian, and *One Mid-Summer's Morning* received its premiere performance in Canada.

Healey, whose total output includes works in most genres, has had over forty works published in the U.K., Canada and the U.S. Five works have been issued on records including his suite *Arctic Images*. Perhaps Healey's most significant achievement to date is the opera *Seabird Island,* which was the first contemporary opera to be taken on a professional cross-Canada tour. His awards include the University of Louisville Second International Composition Contest, and the Delius Festival Composition Award. A singular honor is Healey's inclusion in the 2001 New Grove Music Dictionary of Music and Musicians.

Healey has written about his style and influence: "The first pieces with which I am satisfied were written in the Neo-Classic style, a style which appealed to me coming from an organist's background; the composers I particularly liked were Hindemith and Milhaud. After some four or five years I became concerned with the strict limitations of classicism and this resulted in a period in Italy where I studied the techniques of the Second Viennese and Post-Webern schools. The techniques of these composers have stayed with me ever since as a continuum on which to place other current interests, the most important of these being ethnic music and also techniques learned from electronic music.

"Since I have lived for considerable periods of time in England, Canada and the U.S.A., I am more conscious than most of the effect the environment has upon musical creativity—the effect of which is to divide one's compositions into a number of clearly definable artistic periods. Despite the resulting compartmentalization of one's creative output, I feel that my music has been true to the different artistic worlds in which I have lived—the resulting divergences being an exciting phenomenon of Global Shrinkage and the Immigrant Twentieth Century Composer." (CMC)

One Mid-Summer's Morning: *An English Folk-Set for Wind Band and Percussion*
Difficulty: Grade 6
Duration: 23:00
Composed in 1997
Available through CMC (www.musiccentre.com) and the composer (www.derekhealey.com)

One Mid-Summer's Morning introduces both the player and listener to a special and unique musical landscape. The melodic foreground is made up of lovely English folk songs, but they are dressed in such original colors that the work must be heard aloud to be fully appreciated.

Healey has great affinity for the percussion family, in this case including an important piano part, and it is often given a very evocative role. To perform this work properly, one needs a dedicated percussion section that can rise to a challenge. In general, Healey is sparing in his use of full tuttis, and the style is often pointillistic with much outstanding solo playing. Given the unique color of this music, it is probably one of the most significant works written for band in the last decade, and should be played by all ensembles capable of performing it well. The movements are: *1. Among the New Mown Hay; 2.The Banks of Sweet Primroses; 3. High Germany; 4. Strawberry Fair; 5. Bushes and Briars;* and *6. Shropshire Rounds.* (CMC and Michael Purves-Smith)

This work may be heard on a recording made by the Wellington Winds and available through CMC, "An Artist's Neighbourhood," (Chestnut Hall Music #02003) with Michael Purves-Smith conducting.

JOHN HERBERMAN (B. 1953)

JOHN HERBERMAN COMES TO composing, arranging, and music production via a wide range of musical experiences. Herberman has degrees in Music and in Education from the University of Toronto, as well as extensive training in composition from the Royal Conservatory of Music and with the late Gordon Delamont. He has also done graduate work in film scoring and arranging at the Eastman School of Music. He taught high school music for seven years before leaving the teaching profession to devote all his time to music production. Since that time, Herberman has written and recorded music for film, television, radio, and TV commercials, live theatre and industrial shows, and jazz groups—both vocal and instrumental. He composed original music for *Family Passions* on CTV, *Once Upon a Hamster* for YTV, and created soundscapes for Dan Gibson's acclaimed "Solitudes" series of recordings. Several of his band compositions have been published and receive international distribution. Herberman also has extensive corporate and private market experience as leader/arranger for a successful top-40 dance band and a classical trio.

Herberman has had the distinction of being asked to design the sound and music for two national museums in Ottawa: the National Aviation Museum, and the Canada In Space exhibit in the Museum of Science and Technology. The Aviation Museum produced a one-hour CBC co-production featuring Pierre Berton, which has won several international awards. (© Northdale Music Press, used by permission)

Couchiching Suite
Difficulty: Grade 3
Duration: 7:00
Published 1989 by Comprint

Mr. Herberman wrote this descriptive music while engaged as a composer-in-residence at the National Music Camp at Lake Couchiching north of Toronto in 1989. It consists of three contrasting movements: March (in 5/4), Song (Green Shadows in the Woods), and Molto Allegro. The intriguing modern harmonization and the rhythmical phasing make this a good learning piece and an excellent addition to any program either as single pieces or as a suite. (Fraser Linklater and Comprint Publishing, used by permission)

The Fisher Who Died in His Bed
Difficulty: Grade 4
Duration 12:30 (3:00 + 4:00 + 3:00 + 2:30)
Published 1995 by Northdale Music Press (www.northdalemusic.com)

This charming and expressive work derives its inspiration from the Newfoundland ballad about the demise of East Coast fisherman Jim Jones. Each of the four movements in this suite portrays a contrasting mood. The piece weaves prominent solo clarinet work and strong inner voices together with the entire ensemble to create a haunting aural tapestry. The composer wrote the music while serving as conductor of the Hamilton Concert Band, who premiered it.

The composer first heard this haunting ballad on a tape by the East Coast group Figgy Duff, performed a cappella. After much searching, a complete text was found, with notation. The verses portray the life of Jim Jones, a noted fisherman, who, like all of us, had both 'saintly' and dark traits. It is the chronicling of a folk hero:

> *Old Jim Jones the fisher, the trapper, the trawler,*
> *Jim Jones the fish killin' banker is dead.*
> *No fisherman surely never stepped in a dory,*
> *Like Jim Jones the fisher who died in his bed.*

Herberman's approach is consistently lyrical, even in the last movement, and features beautiful inner lines, highly effective scoring, and the modal harmony that would be expected in folk music. Each movement of this piece segues into the next, and the suite can be played in its entirety without pause or interruption. However, the four movements may also be played individually. The instruments that introduce each movement are indicated with brackets in the score, inserted at the beginning of movements II, III, and IV to indicate the appropriate starting points. The instruments that don't play have corresponding instructions to remain silent. The four movements are entitled: I. *Jim Jones-The Fisher*; II. *Lament*; III. *Celebration*; IV. *Remembrance*. (CMC, Keith Kinder, and Northdale Music Press, used by permission)

The Fisher Who Died in His Bed has been recorded by the University of Toronto Wind Symphony on a CD entitled *Wind Symphony* (Arbordisc UTWS 9701). A recording of this work also is available on the CD "A Lakeshore Concert," by the Lakeshore Concert Band of Montreal, and may be ordered by emailing the band at *lakeshoreconcertband@coolgoose.com*.

J. Scott Irvine (b. 1953)

J. Scott Irvine's compositions and arrangements have been performed and broadcast across Canada, in the U.S. and in Europe. Several have
been recorded for commercial release on various record labels, including RCA
Victor and the Canadian Broadcasting Corporation's SM 5000 series. He has
also been the recipient of commissioning grants from the Ontario Arts Council
and the Laidlaw Foundation, and is an Associate Composer of the Canadian
Music Centre.

Irvine is also active as a performer, and has played tuba with the Canadian
Opera Company Orchestra, the Esprit Orchestra, the Hannaford Street Silver
Band, and in commercial recording studios for many years. He is perhaps best
known for his playing on the acclaimed children's television series Sharon, Lois
and Bram's *Elephant Show.* Highly committed to new music, Irvine has commissioned solo works for the tuba by several noted Canadian composers. (CMC
and Northdale Music Press, used by permission)

Hannaford Overture
Difficulty: Grade 5
Duration: 7:30
Published 1990 by Northdale Music Press (www.northdalemusic.com)

The *Hannaford Overture* is a showpiece full of melody and motion. The main
theme, slower middle section, and reiteration are challenging and interesting to every member of the band. The piece builds effectively to its closing,
leaving a lasting impression of its memorable tune. A solid bass section is
recommended.

Composer's Notes on *Hannaford Overture:*

Hannaford Overture was written for the Hannaford Street Silver Band of
Toronto, Canada in celebration of the International Year of Canadian Music
(1986) and was premièred by them in October of that year under conductor
Wayne Jeffrey. The work is dedicated to the members of the HSSB, who have
performed it across Canada. My intention was to write a light, "audience-
friendly" Canadian concert opener, reminiscent of some of the English and
American band music I enjoyed playing in my formative years. In 1990, at the
urging of several colleagues, I scored a second version of the work for concert
band. (© Northdale Music Press, used by permission)

A recording of the brass band version is available on CD by the Hannaford
Street Silver band, Stephen Chenette, conductor (CBC SMCD 5103).

ANDRE JUTRAS (B. 1961)

BORN AND RAISED IN Québec, Andre Jutras began his musical studies at age eight. He then graduated in oboe and chamber music from the Conservatoire de Musique de Montreal (1979) and went to l'Universite Laval (Québec City) to study composition, analysis and orchestration with Francois Morel.

Between 1985 and 1991, he held the English horn position with l'Orchestre symphonique de Québec, while studying conducting with Simon Streatfeild and Gabriel Chmura. In 1991, he became Staff Conductor with the Calgary Philharmonic Orchestra, a three-year residency that would lead him to conduct between 45 to 50 concerts a year and give him the opportunity to study with Maestro Mario Bernardi and many international guest conductors. In addition to Calgary, he has conducted orchestras in Winnipeg, Edmonton, Québec, Vancouver, Windsor, Thunder Bay and performances of the Alberta Ballet Company.

Besides pursuing a "classical" career, he also played saxophone in jazz bands for many years and conducted concert bands, jazz ensembles and pops orchestras, often performing his own arrangements or compositions. He is a well-known clinician and adjudicator, giving conducting workshops and leading musical groups of all levels.

In 1992 and 1993, he received the "Jean-Marie Baudet Award" from the Canada Council for the Arts as one of Canada's most gifted young conductors.

Since April 2000, he holds the position of Music Officer with the Canada Council for the Arts, dealing with grants to professional orchestras, opera companies, professional choirs and residencies for conductors and composers. (C. L. Barnhouse Company, © Chesford Music Publications; reproduced by permission)

A Barrie North Celebration
Difficulty: Grade 3
Duration: 7:32
Published 1993 by Barnhouse

This work was commissioned by the Music Parents' Association of Barrie North to commemorate the 20th year of music at the school. The Association also had a mandate to support Canadian composers and performers, and commissioning Mr. Jutras allowed them to do both. The Association wanted the piece to have the celebratory feeling of this special anniversary while reflecting the heritage of Simcoe County, where Barrie is located, so they gave Jutras a book on the history of the area. Upon reading the book, he learned that there is a distinct Indian culture in the area, which is also renowned for its scenic and natural history: The Blue Mountains of Collingwood, the ski hills in the surrounding area, the lakes, the farming, and more. Then after collaborating with

Sharon Fitzsimmins, the band director of Barrie North at the time, Mr. Jutras wrote the work to feature solo trumpet and the percussion section in particular. The result is an exciting work with exciting rhythms, beautiful solos, wonderful melodies, and harmonic and rhythmic concepts not often found in traditional band literature. (Sharon Fitzsimmins and C. L. Barnhouse Company. © Chesford Music Publications; reproduced by permission.)

C'est Noel!
Difficulty: Grade 3
Duration: 5:02
Published 1985 by Barnhouse

This Christmas concert piece has enjoyed continuing popularity for more than two decades. Based on three traditional Christmas songs that are well known throughout Canada and the United States, it is structured in a fast/slow/fast form. *C'est Noel!* opens with a brilliant introduction based on *Il est Ne' le Divin Enfant* (He Is Born the Holy Child), then moves to *Sainte Nuit* (Holy Night). The third tune is *Les Anges dans nos campagnes* (Angels We Have Heard on High), with *Joy to the World* used as an upper woodwind counterpoint. *C'est Noel* was commissioned by Mr. Laurent Breton for a special combined band of high school musicians from the Quebec City area, and was premiered on December 5, 1984 in Quebec City. (C. L. Barnhouse Company. © Chesford Music Publications; reproduced by permission.)

Daydreams
Difficulty: Grade 2
Duration: 2:00
Published 1988 by Barnhouse

This beautiful ballad is musically interesting, playable and extremely versatile. Solo parts are written out on the easy and medium grade level, allowing the director to feature a budding superstar. This is an excellent vehicle for young soloists, and an effective teaching device in many respects. (C. L. Barnhouse Company. © Chesford Music Publications; reproduced by permission.)

Inversia
Difficulty: Grade 3
Duration: 6:15
Published 2003 by Barnhouse

This composition from Andre Jutras is a distinctive piece that begins with short expressive solos for flute and clarinet. The contrasting slower section features solos for alto sax and either tenor sax, horn or euphonium before returning to a faster tempo for the exciting ending. (C. L. Barnhouse Company. © Chesford Music Publications; reproduced by permission.)

Latin Sun
Difficulty: Grade 3
Duration: 3:50
Published 1991 by Barnhouse

Latin Sun, a melodic solo for either alto sax, trumpet or flugelhorn with band, is the second movement to Jutras' *Daydreams,* and is intended to be performed as such. Because the grade level and instrumentation of the two works are similar, it will be very easy to program both with the same soloist. This short Latin work will introduce the young soloist to jazz improvisation. Although there is a written jazz solo, Jutras' hope is that soloists will add some improvisational ideas of their own. (C. L. Barnhouse Company. © Chesford Music Publications; reproduced by permission.)

Moventa
Difficulty: Grade 4
Duration: 5:01
Published 1989 by Barnhouse

Moventa is dedicated to the Cobequid Education Center Symphonic Band in Truro, Nova Scotia, Canada, conducted by Ron McKay; and to the memory of Claude T. Smith, whose music and personality were an inspiration to the composer. The opening legato chorale gives way to an allegro con brio characterized by a slight jazz feeling, and features a snare drum and timpani duet that is intended to sound improvised. This composition works well as either a concert opener or closer. (C. L. Barnhouse Company. © Chesford Music Publications; reproduced by permission.)

They Came Sailing
Difficulty: Grade 3
Duration: 4:42
Published 1994 by Barnhouse

Subtitled "Suite Jacques-Cartier", this appealing composition is a suite in one movement and is excellent literature for either concert or contest use. Jacques Cartier was a navigator who made three voyages for France to the North American continent between 1534 and 1542, where he explored the St. Lawrence River and gave Canada its name. This work's fiery and contemporary style reflects the excitement and daring of Cartier's expedition to the New World. This work provides an excellent avenue to teach students about Canadian history and culture. (Encyclopedia Britannica and C. L. Barnhouse Company, © Chesford Music Publications; reproduced by permission.)

A recording of this work is available on the CD "A Lakeshore Concert," by the Lakeshore Concert Band of Montreal, and may be ordered by emailing the band at *lakeshoreconcertband@coolgoose.com.*

Three Folk Miniatures
Difficulty: Grade 3
Duration: 5:20
Published 1986 by Barnhouse

This beautifully rich and diverse work by Canadian composer Andre Jutras may be the most frequently performed of all Canadian works. It is based on well-known French Canadian folksongs that contrast in tempo and style. The first folk song is *V'la l'Bon Vent*, which translates, "Here is the good wind." It is said to have been used by French sailors on their way to discover Canada in the early 17th century. Like many other sea chanties, it was sung to establish a rhythm for hoisting the main sail upon the arrival of a good tailwind. The second, *Isabeau, s'y promene*, is a haunting and sad love song that tells of the loneliness of being away from a loved one. The third folk song is *Les Raftmen*, a well-known folk melody that was sung by the loggers and lumberjacks of the Canadian forests. Its steady rhythm provided a basis for swings of the axe in unison. After the trees were cut down they were dragged to the river and tied into huge floating rafts, and the "raftmen" would ride the log rafts down the river to the sawmill. (Fraser Linklater and C. L. Barnhouse Company. © Chesford Music Publications; reproduced by permission.)

A recording of this work is available on the CD "North Winds—Canadian Wind Band Music," which may be ordered from the University of Manitoba, Faculty of Music, 65 Dafoe Road, Winnipeg, Manitoba, Canada R3T 2N2 or by calling (204) 474-9310. A recording also is available on the CD "A Lakeshore Concert," by the Lakeshore Concert Band of Montreal, and may be ordered by emailing the band at *lakeshoreconcertband@coolgoose.com*.

GARY KULESHA (B. 1954)

GARY KULESHA IS ONE of Canada's most active and most visible musicians. Although principally a composer, he is active as a pianist, conductor, and teacher. He directs the Contemporary Music Ensemble and coordinates the Theory and Composition Department at the University of Toronto, and also is the Composer-Advisor to the Toronto Symphony, where his duties include composing, conducting, and advising on repertoire.

Mr. Kulesha's music has been commissioned, performed, and recorded by musicians and ensembles all over the world. His *Angels for Marimba and Tape* has become a standard repertoire item for percussionists, and receives over a hundred performances per year. *Celebration Overture* is one of the most performed orchestral pieces written in Canada, and *Four Fantastic Landscapes* has entered the repertoire of several noted pianists from Canada and Europe. Mr. Kulesha's first opera, *Red Emma*, was included in Opera America's book of *Operas Which Should Be Performed More Often,* beside works by Copland, Bernstein, and Weill.

In 1988, he was appointed Composer In Residence with the Kitchener-Waterloo Symphony Orchestra, a position he held until 1992. In 1993, he was appointed Composer In Residence with the Canadian Opera Company, a position he held until the end of 1995. His *Symphony* for two conductors and orchestra was awarded a prize at the Winnipeg Symphony New Music Festival in 2001 as Best Canadian Orchestra Composition of the 1990's.

In 1990, Mr. Kulesha was nominated for a JUNO award for his *Third Chamber Concerto.* He was nominated again in 2000 for *The Book of Mirrors.* In 1986, he was named Composer of the Year by PROCanada, the youngest composer ever so honored. Also in 1986, he represented Canada at the International Rostrum of Composers in Paris. In the summer of 1990, he was the first composer ever appointed to the position of Composer In Residence with the Festival of the Sound in Parry Sound, Ontario. He has returned every year since 1996 to direct the Young Composers program at the Festival.

Mr. Kulesha has been the Artistic Director of The Composers' Orchestra since 1987, stepping down in 2004 in favor of three young composers. His conducting activities are extensive, and he has premiered hundreds of works. He has guest conducted frequently with several major orchestras throughout Canada, and has recorded for radio and CD. Although he is well known as a specialist in 20th Century music, his repertoire is extensive, ranging from little-known Baroque music through to the music of our time.

In 2002, Mr. Kulesha was awarded the first National Arts Centre Orchestra Composer Award. This began a four-year relationship with the NACO and its Artistic Director, Pinchas Zuckerman. (CMC and interview with the composer)

Ensembles for Winds
Difficulty: Grade 5
Duration: 9:00
Composed in 1979
Available through CMC (www.musiccentre.ca)

Ensembles was written for the Scarborough Concert Band in 1979 and was commissioned through the Ontario Arts Council. Through a special arrangement with the SCB, the premiere was actually given by Stephen Chenette and the University of Toronto Wind Symphony in March of 1980. The work is in three movements, slow-fast-slow. The title indicates that the scoring emphasizes ensembles within the larger group, and in fact, there is no full tutti anywhere in the piece. The group is not just winds, but includes percussion, piano, and double bass.

The material of the outer two movements begins with chorale-like statements, which are then organically elaborated into larger structures. The third movement opens and closes with "simultaneous musics" from various sections of the ensemble; the materials contrast tonal chords and progressions with polytonal backgrounds. The second movement, for brass, piano and percussion without woodwinds, is rhythmic and fast, beginning with a statement by piano and percussion. There is a brief fugal exposition halfway through the movement, which features the subject matter presented in a Hindemithian version of a jazz "thickened line." The movement closes with the opening material repeated and rounded off. (CMC and interview with the composer)

A pedagogical discussion of this work can be found on page 57 of *Guidelist of Unpublished Canadian Band Music Suitable for Student Performers* by Patricia Martin Shand.

March in F
Difficulty: Grade 3
Duration: 4:30
Composed in 1975
Available through CMC (www.musiccentre.ca)

Commissioned by the Scarborough Concert Band, this composition uses ABA form with the thematic material of the A section introduced by trumpets. The theme is repeated and developed, passing to other sections in the ensemble. A D.S. al fine leads to a repeat of the A section. The tempo is marked at 108, and should not drag. This work is especially helpful in teaching dynamics and ensemble balance and blend. (Patricia Shand)

A pedagogical discussion of this work can be found on page 22 of *Guidelist of Unpublished Canadian Band Music Suitable for Student Performers* by Patricia Martin Shand.

Overture for Concert Band
Difficulty: Grade 5
Duration: 9:00
Composed in 1983
Available through CMC (www.musiccentre.ca)

This overture was commissioned by the Scarborough Concert Band through the Ontario Arts Council. The work features the development of clearly stated melodic material with considerable variety of texture from solo instruments to full ensemble. Solo flute, oboe, clarinet, and bassoon are featured prominently, and the percussion section will enjoy a solo passage as well. The outer movements are marked at 86, while the middle section is faster at quarter note = 128. Subtle tempo changes and complex rhythmic patterns create additional interest for the players. This grade 5 work provides opportunities to develop both technical skills and ensemble sensitivity and fluency as musical lines pass from one section to another. (Patricia Shand)

A pedagogical discussion of this work can be found on page 58 of *Guidelist of Unpublished Canadian Band Music Suitable for Student Performers* by Patricia Martin Shand.

Two Pieces for Band
Difficulty: Grade 2
Duration: ca. 7:00
Composed in 1982
Available through CMC (www.musiccentre.ca)

Commissioned by the Alliance for Canadian New Music Projects through the Ontario Arts Council, *Two Pieces for Band* was written in part to introduce young musicians to 20th century compositional techniques. The work includes modern concepts of harmony, rhythm, and notation without being too difficult for the players to grasp.

The first movement, *March*, is based on dissonance and syncopation. The second, *Through Morning Mist*, is programmatic and scored almost entirely in graphic notation requiring controlled improvisation. A gradually building texture that includes birdcalls and non-pitched sounds eventually arrives at an F major chord to depict the rising of the sun. (CMC and Keith Kinder)

A pedagogical discussion of this work can be found on page 23 of *Guidelist of Unpublished Canadian Band Music Suitable for Student Performers* by Patricia Martin Shand.

ALFRED KUNZ (B. 1929)

ALFRED KUNZ IS A noted Canadian composer, choirmaster, conductor, arranger, and music publisher. Mr. Kunz was born in Neudorf, Saskatchewan in 1929 of German parentage. His early music studies took place first in Kitchener, Ontario and then in Toronto. Later, as a teenager in Ontario, he told his friends he was going to be a composer, before he even "knew what a composer was." Since his youth he has had a significant impact on the musical heritage and culture of the local community. Following this he spent from 1964–65 studying composition and conducting in Germany (Staatsexamen, Mainz). Upon his return to Canada he was appointed Director of Music at the University of Waterloo, where he remained until 1979.

Since leaving the University he has been working as a free agent, composing, arranging and conducting. In 1980 he formed his own music publishing house.

Although his major creative output has been choral, his music covers all genres of writing. Since 1980 he has written numerous works for orchestra, concert band, string orchestra and choral music for school use. Compared to his early writing, Kunz has settled on a more conservative style.

Today, Kunz has seen many of his childhood dreams come true. He has composed numerous original works, including orchestral and chamber music, operas and operettas, oratorios, choral works and many songs. His expert musical stewardship has allowed many individuals across Canada to experience the joy of making, as well as listening to, music: classical, contemporary, folk, and sacred. (CMC)

Canadian Trilogy
Difficulty: Grade 4
Duration: 7:00
Published 1982 by A. Kunz Music (www.kunzmusic.ca)

Canadian Trilogy was composed to fill a need for concert band arrangements of Canadian folk songs. In character the music is written in a straightforward manner with obbligato and contrapuntal lines to give the work sparkle, verve, and rhythmic interest. The trilogy uses three Canadian folk songs from three of Canada's "musical" provinces: 1. *The Banks of Newfoundland*, an exciting folk song; 2. *Un Canadian Errant* (Once a Canadian Lad), a quasi love song from Québec written in a "soft shoe" manner; and 3. *Nova Scotia Song*, which is march-like in character and brings the trilogy to a close. (Interview with the composer)

ROBERT LEMAY (B. 1960)

ROBERT LEMAY TEACHES THEORY, form and analysis, and composition at Laurentian University in Sudbury, Ontario. An award-winning composer, he holds a doctoral degree in composition from the Université de Montréal with Michel Longtin and a masters degree from Université Laval with François Morel. Lemay also studied at the State University of New York at Buffalo with David Felder and has taken part in seminars with Brian Ferneyhough, Louis Andriessen, and Donald Erb.

Among his recent honors is the second prize from the Kazimierz Serocki 10th International Composers' Competition 2006, a prestigious international orchestra contest in Poland organized by the Polish Society for Contemporary Music. Other international prizes include the first prize from the 2004 Harelbeke Muziekstad Wind Ensemble Competition in Belgium. The first prize was given by the city of Harelbeke with 10,000 Euro for his piece, *Ramallah* for alto saxophone and wind ensemble. In addition, Lemay received the first prize at the Fourth Contrabassoon Composers Competition "El Ruiseñor Grave" in Buenos Aires, Argentina in 1998, three prizes from the CAPAC (presently SOCAN), and received numerous grants from the Quebec, the Ontario, and the Canada Council for the Arts.

His music, which often employs virtuoso performance techniques, is characterized by an imaginative and unconventional use of the concert hall space. Lemay has composed many works, and his music has been performed internationally. Many of his pieces have also been broadcast on Radio-Canada, the CBC, Bavarian State Radio and Polish National Radio. By 2006, his music had been released commercially on six different CDs, including "Débâcle" on the Atma label by Estria Woodwind Quintet. His piece *Mitsu no kisetsu* for mezzo-soprano and baritone saxophone is published by the Éditions Jobert in Paris. Four pieces for solo saxophone, including the 5 Études for alto saxophone, are also published by the Éditions Fuzeau in France. Saxophone is dominant in his entire oeuvre, and Lemay has written for numerous international performers. Most recently, Lemay wrote a piano concert for the Japanese-Canadian pianist Yoko Hirota, premiered by the Sudbury Symphony Orchestra.

He is a member of the Canadian League of Composers and the Canadian Music Centre, both of which require extensive peer review for membership. He is also the President and the Co-artistic director of the 5-Penny New Music Concerts in Sudbury. (CMC and Laurentian University)

Apeldoorm, Nederland
Difficulty: Grade 6
Duration: 10:54
Composed in 2006
Available through CMC (www.musiccentre.ca)

The composer writes, "During a trip to the Netherlands in the 1990s, I was surprised to discover that the Dutch continue to honor Canadians, whose soldiers liberated their country during World War II. Since then I have not looked at our war veterans with the same eyes. *Apeldoorm, Nederland* is also inspired by Guillaume Apollinaire's poem, "Liens" ("Bonds"), published in *Calligrammes. Poems of Peace and War* (1918). The poet served in World War I and wrote a number of poems in the trenches."

"Liens" is a work of concrete poetry, in which the typographical arrangement of words is as important in conveying the intended effect as the conventional elements of the poem, such as meaning of words, rhythm, rhyme and so on. Although a translation of such a work fails to convey its full meaning, below is a translation of the extract of this poem that appears in the score:

> Cords made of cries
> Sounds of bells through Europe
> Hanging centuries
> Rails binding the nations
> We are only two or three men
> Free of all chains
> Let's join hands
> Violent rain combing the smoke

This challenging, delicate, and evocative atonal work reflects the composer's view of the war. The work was a finalist for the First Tokyo Kosei Wind Orchestra Composition Competition in Tokyo, Japan in 2006, and was recorded by that ensemble. All players must be highly accomplished and the percussion section must be quite versatile, as the score calls for more than 20 percussion instruments, including numerous drums, gongs and cymbals. (Interview with the composer)

RON MACKAY (B. 1928)

RON MACKAY STUDIED CONDUCTING with Ifan Williams at the Maritime Conservatory of Music and French horn with Keith Vernon and Reginald Barrow of the Detroit and Toronto Symphony Orchestras. He graduated as a bandmaster from the Canadian Forces School of Music in 1959 and served as principal hornist, then bandmaster of several navy bands. He also held the position of music director at Pt. Edward Naval Base, Royal Canadian Sea Cadets. Mr. MacKay organized the Nova Scotia Provincial Band (non-competition) Festival and Workshop in 1973, the Atlantic Stage Band Festival in 1975 and again in 1978–79, and the Maritime Music Festival in 1986 and 1989. In 1970 he began teaching and directing the bands at the Cobequid Educational Center in Truro, Nova Scotia. The center's symphonic band, formed in 1966, has appeared throughout the Maritimes, in Ontario and Quebec, in Bermuda, England, and the USA. In 1989 MacKay became conductor of the Scotia Wind Ensemble in Halifax, and also president of the Canadian Band Association. In his "retirement" he continues to conduct, consult, and write music for young bands. (The Canadian Encyclopedia and Jeff Reynolds)

Jim
Difficulty: Grade 2
Duration: 3:30
Composed in 2004
Available from the composer (email info@buckleymusic.com)

In December 2003 Nova Scotia lost a supremely talented and dear friend, Jim Hargreaves. The composer wrote this stirring work in his memory. The Nova Scotia Youth Wind Ensemble premiered it in 2004 in New Glasgow. *Jim* is a lyrical work that features solo opportunities for horn and trumpet, and is an excellent work to use in teaching phrasing and the importance of the musical line. (Denise Grant)

Arnold MacLaughlan

Arnold MacLaughlan is a long-time music teacher and music consultant in the St. George area near Quebec. In the tradition of Holst, Vaughan Williams, Grainger, and many others, MacLaughlan has adapted folk songs to the wind band medium. He published a number of band methods, but is best known for his excellent *A French-Canadian Suite.*

A French-Canadian Suite
Difficulty: Grade 1+
Duration: 3:40
Published 1987 by Bourne

If Darius Milhaud had written for very young band, it might have sounded like this three movement work. Quebec has a strong folk music tradition, and Quebec composer MacLaughlin captures this tradition beautifully in this arrangement. Movement 1, *Joli Tambour,* about a drummer boy, is an excellent piece to teach the art of accenting. Movement 2, *C'est la Belle Françoise,* a song describing a soldier's farewell to his fiancée, would be an excellent work to teach legato tonguing. The lively third movement, *A St. Malo, Beau Port de Mer,* is based on the story of French Explorer Jacques Cartier, one of Canada's early "founding fathers," who set sail in 1534 on a voyage of discovery from the Normandy port of St. Malo. In this work all instruments go above the average grade 1 range, and all instruments except the bells have a statement of the melodic line. (Fraser Linklater)

A recording of this work is available on the CD "North Winds—Canadian Wind Band Music," which may be ordered from the University of Manitoba, Faculty of Music, 65 Dafoe Road, Winnipeg, Manitoba, Canada R3T 2N2 or by calling (204) 474-9310.

SCOTT MACMILLAN (B. 1955)

SCOTT MACMILLAN, BORN IN Halifax, Nova Scotia, is recognized as one of Canada's leading musicians, and for playing an integral role in widening the audience for the music of Atlantic Canada both nationally and internationally.

He completed a Bachelor of Arts in Mathematics at Halifax's Dalhousie University, where he also took courses in music, and continued his musical training at Humber College in Toronto. During his school years he worked as a guitar player and subsequently spent five years as a touring musician. His Scott Macmillan Sextet was a winner in the Atlantic region for his original compositions in the Alcan Montreal Jazz Festival in 1987.

Equally at home on the podium, in the studio or behind a guitar, Macmillan is in great demand as a music director, performer/conductor, arranger and producer. He has composed for film, television and radio, and has created commissioned works for Mermaid Theater, Symphony Nova Scotia, St. Cecelia Concert Series, and Scotia Festival. An exceptional guitarist, Macmillan has been nominated seven times for ECMA awards, receiving the Instrumental Artist of the Year Award in 1998, Best Classical Recording for *MacKinnon's Brook Suite* in 2002 and *Bach Meets Cape Breton* with a "Puirt a Baroque" in 1995.

Macmillan's interest in composing and conducting deepened following master classes with Victor Yampolsky and participation in a CBC National Arrangers Workshop. His expertise in and understanding of regional folk and Celtic music led him to compose initially for his Celtic-crossover group, The Octet. This in turn led to the first of many commissions, *The Celtic Mass for the Sea* for CBC Maritimes, which he co-wrote with librettist Jennyfer Brickenden. Since its premiere in 1991, the *Celtic Mass for the Sea* has been performed annually throughout Canada, and was cheered by audiences at its New York premiere in June of 2002 at Carnegie Hall and at its European premiere in July 2004. Macmillan has received a number of awards from the Canada Council for the Arts and the Nova Scotia Arts Partnership, including the creation in 2002/03 of his first symphony, *SUMMUS*, a musical exploration of palindromes, supported by the Canada Council.

He is well known for his work with Symphony Nova Scotia, with whom he has been Host Conductor of the Maritime Pops Series since 1995. His musical collaborations have contributed significantly to the exploding Atlantic pop music scene since the mid-1980s. His work with Atlantic artists has led to conducting and programming engagements with other major orchestras, including the National Arts Centre Orchestra, the Kitchener-Waterloo Symphony, the Vancouver Symphony, the Calgary Philharmonic, the Winnipeg Symphony, and the Royal Scottish National Orchestra.

In 2001 Mr. Macmillan created a new work for orchestra, bagpipes and tin whistles entitled *MacKinnon's Brook Suite*, capturing the immigrant story of Scottish settlers to Cape Breton. This work won the 2002 East Coast Music

Award (ECMA) for Best Classical Recording, and premiered as a television special on CBC's Opening Night in January of 2003.

Mr. Macmillan is on the Board of the Guild of Canadian Film Composers, and is a member of Canadian League of Composers, an Associate Composer of the Canadian Music Centre, the Atlantic Canadian Composers Association, the Society of Composers, Authors and Music Publishers of Canada (SOCAN), and the Atlantic Federation of Musicians. His contribution to the cultural life of Atlantic Canada was recognized by the University College of Cape Breton, which awarded him an honorary Doctor of Letters degree in 1997. (CMC)

Cheticamp Overture
Difficulty: Grade 3
Duration: 6:00
Published 2001 by Scojen Music Production Ltd. (email scojen@ns.sympatico.ca)

This work was commissioned by the Stadacona Band of the Maritime Command in Halifax, Nova Scotia (Canada's east coast navy band), and is based on Acadian folk songs. The Acadians were French settlers of eastern Canada who were exiled from their land by the British in the 1750s because of their refusal to swear allegiance to England. (The Cajuns are their descendants who settled in Louisiana.) Cheticamp is an Acadian community on the west coast of Cape Breton, rich in the culture of Acadian folk songs.

Cheticamp Overture begins with a stately hymn and then goes into two up-beat songs. At the end the work recaps the hymn and concludes in grand fashion. A recording of the overture is available on a CD by the Stadacona Band entitled "On the Quarterdeck," catalog number BNA 5113. (CMC, The Canadian Encyclopedia, and interview with the composer)

Twelve in Five
Difficulty: Grade 5
Duration: 5:00
Published 1992 by Scojen Music Production Ltd. (email scojen@ns.sympatico.ca)

Twelve in Five was commissioned by the Stadacona Band of the Maritime Command in Halifax, Nova Scotia (the navy band stationed in Halifax), and premiered by that ensemble in July 1993. It was written in commemoration of the 125th birthday of Canada in the year 1992. The title derives from the fact that in 1992 Canada had ten provinces and two territories, giving the country at that time twelve distinct sections. However, on April 1, 1999 Nunavut became a territory and changed the map of Canada for the first time in half a century.

The work is an up-beat samba, primarily in 5/4 meter, thus connecting to the title. The melody plays the 1, 2, and 5 notes of the home key; and then 1, 2, 6 and 1, 2, 7 respectively, thus subliminally looking forward to the future growth of Canada. (CMC and interview with the composer)

DAVID MARLATT (B. 1973)

DAVID MARLATT IS A trumpet player who obtained a music education degree from the University of Western Ontario, Canada. He was principal cornet in the Whitby Brass Band for 6 years and founder of the trumpet ensemble "Trumpets in Style." As a performer, he has played in jazz bands, brass quintets, orchestras, concert bands, brass bands and period instrument ensembles.

Mr. Marlatt has composed pieces for concert band, string orchestra, brass quintet, trumpet ensemble, piano, tuba and trumpet. His writing style is diverse and he has been commissioned to write for a wide range of difficulty levels from very young concert band to professional brass quintet. His jazz based trumpet ensemble pieces, *Groovy Vamp* and *A Coconut Named Alex* have been well received by audiences everywhere and his concert band compositions are found on many contest lists.

He has also arranged over 600 pieces of repertoire from the Renaissance to the Romantic eras, such as Monteverdi madrigals, a large suite of music from Handel's *Messiah,* Largo from *New World Symphony* and even Mahler's *Symphony No. 1.* His compositions and arrangements have been played by many performers around the world including Erik Schultz, The Canadian Brass and New York Brass quintets, Toronto Festive Brass, Brassroots, Matthias Hofs, Alaska Brass, Hannaford Street Silver Band and many elementary and secondary school concert bands. (© Eighth Note Publications, used by permission)

Concord Fanfare
Difficulty: Grade 2
Duration: 1:45
Published 2004 by Eighth Note Publications (www.enpmusic.com)

This short, energetic work contains all the elements one would expect in a fanfare. Running scale passages in the upper woodwinds, driving percussion parts and fanfares in the brass make this an interesting concert opener, yet all parts are playable by young bands. The lower voices have scalar runs that give them interesting lines to play. (© Eighth Note Publications, used by permission)

Crimond
Difficulty: Grade 2+
Duration: 3:02
Published by Eighth Note Publications (www.enpmusic.com)

Crimond is perhaps better known as the hymn tune *The Lord is My Shepherd.* This elegant arrangement begins with an inventive brass quartet statement before continuing with the tutti scoring more commonly used in writing for young band. The melody is passed from section to section, adding rhythmic variations to build interest. The work finishes with dissonance in the lower voices, resolving to a powerful and dramatic major chord. (Fraser Linklater and Eighth Note Publications, used by permission)

Festival of Lights
Difficulty: Grade 3
Duration: 5:45
Published 2000 by Eighth Note Publications (www.enpmusic.com)

This energetic composition is the composer's homage to some of his favorite compositions and composers such as John Cheetham, John Barnes Chance and the great Alfred Reed. Short musical quotations and suggestive melodic or rhythmic passages are included in the framework of this piece. The majority of the material is original and the rhythms, lyrical themes and jazz-like harmonies are all elements that reflect the composer's musical influences. (© Eighth Note Publications, used by permission)

Markham Fair Suite
Difficulty: Grade 2
Duration: 5:50
Published 1998 by Eighth Note Publications (www.enpmusic.com)

This set of short pieces depicts events that occur annually at fairs all across North America. Ferris wheels, cotton candy, and a fanfare to open the fair are all included. Unique to this short suite is *Old McDonald's Barn,* a popular viewing event with children found at the Markham Fair. In this movement, animal noises are emulated within the group. Every section in the band gets a chance to perform some melodic material. (© Eighth Note Publications, used by permission)

O Canada
Difficulty: Four separate grades: 1, 1 1/2, 2, 3
Duration: 1:05 per version
Published by Eighth Note Publications (www.enpmusic.com)

Over the years there have been surprisingly few arrangements of the national anthem of Canada. This version is quite unique and will prove to be extremely useful in all kinds of performance situations. This is an arrangement for four levels of difficulty, and the conductor may select the version best suited to the ensemble. All four versions can be found in everyone's part:

1. Unison—this edition has been transposed into a comfortable range for all players.
2. Grade 1 1/2—in this version the melody passes through several sections in a very playable arrangement.

3. Grade 2—more complex moving lines are introduced.
4. Grade 3—this utilizes fanfares in the trumpets and places more range and technical demands on all players.

All these versions are in the same key and use the same basic harmonies, making them completely interchangeable. This revolutionary concept means that elementary schools and high schools can own the same set and combine players for a mass band concert. This set of arrangements is ideal for any program regardless of the diversity of talents. (© Eighth Note Publications, used by permission)

Reesor Park
Difficulty: Grade 1
Duration: 4:50
Published 2002 by Eighth Note Publications (www.enpmusic.com)

Reesor Park, written for the young musicians of Reesor Park Public School in Markham, Ontario (grades 7 and 8), is an energetic overture with rhythmic drive and interest for all players. The composer has written meaningfully for growing bands, and his command of orchestration results in an interesting work that does not "talk down" to young players.

A majestic opening leads to a driving section with shifting rhythms and colorful percussion. The gentle slow section brings a sense of calm, and the piece drives toward an exciting ending. The composer relies on flutes, first trumpet and first alto saxophone, and also gives five percussion players a vital role. Occasional mixed meters and sprung rhythms will provide material to teach these concepts. (Keith Kinder and Eighth Note Publications, used by permission)

Woodcrest Overture
Difficulty: Grade 1
Duration: 3:40
Published 2000 by Eighth Note Publications (www.enpmusic.com)

This original composition is designed to teach both syncopation and the importance of rhythmic precision. It is designed in layers, with each layer stated throughout the composition. Then all the various melodic themes are placed one on top of another to bring the piece to an exciting conclusion. (© Eighth Note Publications, used by permission)

WILLIAM MCCAULEY (1917–1999)

WILLIAM A. MCCAULEY RECEIVED his Bachelor of Music degree at the University of Toronto in 1947 and in the same year became an Associate of the Toronto Conservatory of Music. He received his Master of Music degree at the Eastman School of Music, University of Rochester, New York in 1959. The following year he continued his studies in composition with Alan Hovhaness, Bernard Rogers, and Howard Hanson and in conducting (in Maine) with Pierre Monteux, to earn a Doctor of Musical Arts at Eastman.

He also was principal trombone with the National Film Board and Ottawa Philharmonic orchestras. After completing his doctorate he was house music director 1960–87 of the O'Keefe Centre in Toronto. Concurrently, he was music director 1961–69 at York University, and the York University Choir under his direction won the 1967 City of Lincoln Trophy. Canada's centennial year also saw performances of McCauley's *Fantasy on Canadian Folk Songs* on Parliament Hill. As well, McCauley was music director at Seneca College 1970–78 and conductor of the North York Symphony Orchestra 1972–88. After retirement, he stayed on as conductor emeritus and member of the board.

During his career McCauley composed the scores for more than 125 films, some of which he also conducted. He also wrote music for commercials, and conducted more than 200 recording sessions for films, television, and recordings. In 1998, the Society of Composers, Authors and Music Publishers of Canada honored him with its first Lifetime Achievement Award for Film and Television Music.

Early in his career McCauley developed the adaptable and eclectic style necessary for incidental composition, and he remained a composer without a school. Folk tunes figure in several of his orchestral works, as do elements of jazz. The *Five Miniatures for Flute and Strings* (1958) and the *Concerto Grosso* (1973), both neoclassical, are lyrical and rhythmic. In his music generally dissonance is counteracted by appealing rhythms, cohesive counterpoint, and an uncomplicated sense of direction. Some of his short piano pieces have been used as pedagogical material. In the 1990's McCauley continued to work as a freelance composer and conductor. He was an associate of the Canadian Music Centre. (CMC and The Canadian Encyclopedia)

Canadian Folk Song Fantasy
Difficulty: Grade 5
Duration: 5:16
Published 1972 by Southern

This work is one of the outstanding music products of the Canadian Centennial of 1967. This appealing and well-written collection of Canadian folk songs was commissioned by the Ottawa School Board to commemorate Canada's centennial, and made its premiere on May 22, 1967, on CBC television. It employs some twenty tunes, including at least one from each province, but accompaniment figures hint at many more. Many, but not all, are named in the score.

McCauley has provided lovely countermelodies, effective motivic development, clever canonic textures, and, at times, a profusion of meter changes. Other forms of counterpoint also appear, with as many as three complete songs presented simultaneously. The compositional technique employed in this work is considerably more sophisticated than is normally seen in a medley. (CMC, Keith Kinder, and The Canadian Encyclopedia of Music)

A pedagogical discussion of this work can be found on page 114 of *Canadian Music: A Selective Guidelist for Teachers* by Patricia Martin Shand.

Metropolis
Difficulty: Grade 4
Duration: 6:30
Published 1967 by Oxford Music Press

Originally titled *Big City Suite,* this programmatic suite is descriptive of a bustling city, and features syncopated rhythms, mixed meters, challenging percussion, and many sound effects. The three contrasting movements are: *1. City Hall Ceremony; 2. Lonesome Newcomer; and 3. Rush Hour.* This is an excellent example of program music. (CMC and Patricia Shand)

A pedagogical discussion of this work can be found on page 115 of *Canadian Music: A Selective Guidelist for Teachers* by Patricia Martin Shand.

PIERRE MERCURE (1927–1966)

PIERRE MERCURE, WHO DIED tragically in an automobile accident on January 22, 1966, initially studied piano and later cello, trumpet, flute, organ and bassoon. In addition to his musical activities, he took demanding programs in mathematics and philosophy in a French classical college. While still at college, he enrolled at the Montréal Conservatory and concentrated mainly on bassoon with the idea of playing in an orchestra. In 1946, he was hired as a bassoonist for the Montréal Symphony Orchestra. He played there for about four years, also studying composition at the Conservatory with Claude Champagne.

His first important work was a "symphonic fantasy" entitled *Kaléidoscope,* which has become, since 1948, one of the most frequently played works in the Canadian repertoire. In 1948, Mercure completed another work, *Pantomime,* which is the best illustration of the composer's intention to develop a personal, independent style while remaining musically "objective," that is, by the study of contrasts in the lines, and the examination of form and new sonorities. What one finds here also is an outside influence, and a very strong one, of the painter Paul-Emile Borduas.

In 1949, a Québec government grant enabled him to pursue his studies in Paris with Nadia Boulanger. In 1952, Mercure was asked to produce music programs for the CBC French television network, and he created the very successful television series "L'heure du concert".

The central core around which Mercure's work has developed is an ongoing search for new forms and the need to leave behind the bounds of the conventional so as to discover new worlds of sonorities, such as electronic and musique concrète. This has been his approach from the time of his earliest compositions. For Mercure, "the artist, the composer must be sincere in his presentation of our new era. He must play his role in this continually developing world. The artist must choose: make that world his or escape from it." (CMC and The Canadian Encyclopedia)

Pantomime
Difficulty: Grade 5
Duration: 5:45
Composed in 1949
Published 1971 by Ricordi
Available through CMC (www.musiccentre.ca)

Stylistically rooted in the modern era and written early in Mercure's career for orchestral winds and percussion, it is one of the first works by a Canadian for a wind ensemble other than a band. This fine composition marks the very beginnings of Canadian wind ensemble literature, and has the added distinction of being conducted not only by Zubin Mehta with the Montreal Symphony but also in Carnegie Hall by Leopold Stokowski.

Inspired by the abstract paintings of Québec artist Paul-Emile Borduas and often used as ballet music, this neoclassical, arch-shaped work (ABCBA) has a slow introduction, a fast middle section with a danceable bouncing rhythm, and a slow closing that reflects the opening. The work is somewhat tonal since it is related to the tonality of D, but both the major and minor modes are mixed together. The three movements are marked Peaceful, Lively, and Gracious. There were no program notes written for this piece, but it was often used by choreographers in dances suggesting the awakening of a dancer who expresses the joy of life. The dancer awakes, participates cheerfully in several different dances, and then slowly returns to sleep. (CMC, Denise Grant, Keith Kinder, and Timothy Maloney)

WILLIAM A. MIGHTON (B. 1954)

MR. MIGHTON, A GRADUATE of the Faculty of Music at the University of Toronto, currently teaches music and runs a busy extra-curricular high school music program in the Beaches area of Toronto, Ontario. His "military music" career began when he joined the Band of The Royal Regiment of Canada as a trombonist in 1984, and continues with his current appointment as Director of Music, a position he has held since 1998. Being a member of a regiment whose Colonel-in-Chief is none other than His Royal Highness The Prince Charles, Prince of Wales, Mr. Mighton has had the opportunity to travel extensively in North America and in Europe, and perform for numerous heads of state and other dignitaries. (© Eighth Note Publications, used by permission)

Fields of Honour
Difficulty: Grade 3
Duration: 4:40
Published 2002 by Eighth Note Publications (www.enpmusic.com)

This work is dedicated to the men and women of the Canadian armed forces reserve. Musically, *Fields of Honour* draws its inspiration from some of the military and cultural traditions that have shaped Canadian history. The melodies of the first section are derived from the Canadian national anthem and are meant to recall the Canadian's English heritage. The 6/8 rhythms of the middle section evoke Canadian folk traditions, and the finale combines all these elements in a spirited conclusion. The idea for this march originated from a conversation that took place in the pine forests of Camp Borden, Ontario, during Basic Recruit Course with the Canadian Armed Forces. The composer listened as one of his instructors spoke passionately about the possibility of a new kind of army, an army that would bring peace to the world rather than war. And even though the day when that goal is truly accomplished still lies, unfortunately, sometime in the future, it is true that the honorable role of peacekeeping has now become a major focus of both Reserve and Regular Armed Forces in Canada. This march is an excellent vehicle to teach the concept of hemiola, as many passages feature 2 against 3. (© Eighth Note Publications, used by permission)

Vernon Murgatroyd (B. 1941)

Acclaimed Canadian composer of over 150 orchestral, chamber, choral, vocal, piano, and organ works, Vernon Murgatroyd is also a highly sought piano accompanist to instrumentalists and singers in stage productions and music festivals, as well as a very talented organist.

Mr. Murgatroyd received his Bachelor of Music from the University of Alberta in 1965, with his major being piano and his minor being clarinet. He later focused on composition and began teaching piano, and earned the equivalent of a Master's degree in independent study. Upon graduation and until 1968, he worked as a teacher aid and accompanist-in-residence for various Catholic schools in Bonnyville, Alberta. Since 1968 he has worked as a professional accompanist at the Red Deer Kiwanis Music Festivals.

Mr. Murgatroyd began teaching privately in 1968, and he continues to do this in Red Deer, Alberta today. He was a band instructor at four different Catholic schools from 1973–78, and a recorder instructor at CFB Penhold in Alberta from 1975–78. Following his brief stint there as instructor, he was organist at Trinity Chapel on the Penhold Air Base from 1978 until it closed in 1991.

Mr. Murgatroyd is an associate composer of the Canadian Music Centre and is also a member of the Edmonton Composers' Concert Society (ECCS). He was treasurer of the Alberta Registered Music Teachers' Association and was also a public relations officer for the Red Deer Chamber Music Society.

Mr. Murgatroyd has won several awards, including the Red Deer, Alberta Centennial Award, the Crowsnest Pass Music Award in Composition, and the Red Deer and District Allied Arts Council Celebration of the Arts Award. The latter was awarded for "outstanding accomplishment in music as a composer and performer."

He has been commissioned seven times over his long career, although many players have asked him to write music for them without actually commissioning him. In May 2001, a concert was given in honor of his 60th birthday, during which many of his works were performed. (CMC and interview with the composer)

Red Deer Overture No. 2: Op. 100
Difficulty: Grade 3
Duration: 9:00
Composed in 1984
Available through CMC (www.musiccentre.ca)

The *Red Deer Overture No. 2* received its premiere in March, 1985 in Red Deer, Alberta by The "Perfect Fifth" Lindsay Thurbur Comprehensive High School Band, conducted by Ted Isenor. The band asked Murgatroyd to write something for them, and he responded with this optimistic one-movement work reflecting the future of the town of Red Deer. The 6/8 introduction is followed by a lively tarantella, which leads to a chorale-like *andante maestoso*. The finale is marked "Adagio molto maestoso e marziale," beginning with drum rolls and trumpet fanfares, and building of instrumental groups. Chimes and timpani join to create a satisfying conclusion. (Interview with the composer)

PHIL NIMMONS (B. 1923)

IN A BRILLIANT CAREER spanning six decades, jazz musician, composer and educator Phil Nimmons has made an indelible contribution to the cultural life of Canada. He was named an Officer of the Order of Canada, one of the nation's highest civilian honors, for bringing jazz into the mainstream of music in Canada through radio performances, concerts and workshops with his group "Nimmons 'N' Nine" and other groups. Best known in the early part of his career as a jazz clarinetist, bandleader, composer and arranger, he has also been a tireless advocate of jazz as a significant North American art form. He has been a key figure in Canadian music education, always willing to help and encourage other musicians, particularly those just beginning their studies and careers.

Born in Kamloops, British Columbia, he graduated in pre-medicine from the University of British Columbia before taking up music studies at the Juilliard School of Music in New York and later at the Royal Conservatory of Music in Toronto.

A founding member of the Canadian League of Composers in 1950, he co-founded the Advanced School of Contemporary Music (1960) with Oscar Peterson and the late Ray Brown. Mr. Nimmons was a major influence on the establishment of the Jazz Studies Program at the University of Toronto, where he taught music for 30 years and is now professor emeritus.

His music is familiar to thousands of Canadians and internationally, thanks largely to his performances on his own CBC Radio show beginning in 1953 and as clarinetist and bandleader with his jazz group, Nimmons 'N' Nine, which he later expanded to Nimmons 'N' Nine Plus Six. Nimmons received the first JUNO Award ever given in the jazz category for his group's recording of *The Atlantic Suite,* and also was awarded the first Toronto Arts Award for Music.

In addition to over 400 original jazz compositions and countless arrangements, Mr. Nimmons has written numerous contemporary chamber and orchestral works for voice, piano, strings and other ensembles. His work includes commissions for Expo '67, UNESCO World Music Week, the 1976 World Olympics, and the 1988 Winter Olympics; he has composed scores for stage, film, radio and television and has made a dozen recordings, most recently Sands of Time (2001). The International Association for Jazz Educators named him to its Jazz Education Hall of Fame, and in October 2002 he was presented with the Governor General's Performing Arts Awards for lifetime artistic achievement.

At a point in his career where others might be enjoying retirement, Phil Nimmons continues to work with energy and commitment as a composer, performer and educator. "I'm not fussy about retiring," he says; "It's a word I have trouble spelling, let alone accepting!" He is currently Director Emeritus of Jazz Studies at the University of Toronto and, among other recent engagements, performed at the Ottawa International Jazz Festival and the Stratford Festival's fiftieth anniversary celebrations. (CMC, The Order of Canada, Institute for Canadian Music, and The Canadian Encyclopedia)

Riverscape
Difficulty: Grade 5
Duration: 11:00
Composed in 1994
Available through CMC (www.musiccentre.ca)

Riverscape was a commission from the Fredericton High School Band with assistance from the Canada Council during Canada's 125th birthday celebration in 1994. The band and its conductor, Hugh Kennedy, wanted to add a new work to the body of repertoire that is accessible to school bands. The result is this musical portrait of the Saint John River, which is very much a part of Fredericton and, through its many moods, affects all who live in the city in one way or another. The character of the river was the motivating source for Nimmons' creative process. (Interview with the composer)

Skyscape: *Sleeping Beauty and the Lions*
Difficulty: Grade 5
Duration: 7:50
Composed in 1986
Available through CMC (www.musiccentre.ca)

Skyscape was commissioned for "The Canada Band Project" by the Northdale Concert Band through the Ontario Arts Council. In response to the lack of Canadian band music for special occasions, the band commissioned six of Canada's most accomplished composers to create works for Northdale to perform. On Canada Day, July 1, 1986, the band performed the world premiere of the entire collection at Expo '86. *Skyscape* weaves jazz and classical influences to create an atmospheric portrait of Vancouver, city and mountain scenes. Dramatic, lyrical, and evocative in the hands of an accomplished conductor, this work will both challenge and enchant the band and audience. (Interview with the composer)

A recording of this work is available on the CD "Dreaming on the 2238," (Arbordisc UTWS 9501) by the University of Toronto Wind Symphony.

MICHAEL PARKER (B. 1948)

MICHAEL PARKER WAS BORN in Toronto. He studied violin and viola at the Royal Conservatory of Music in Toronto, in Banff and at Michigan State University. Parker graduated in 1972 with a Masters degree in Classical Studies (Greek and Latin) from the University of Toronto and completed his Ph.D. in Roman Studies from McMaster University in 1991.

In 1976, Parker moved to Newfoundland where he served as principal violist with the Newfoundland Symphony. The following year he was appointed to the faculty of Sir Wilfred Grenfell College, Memorial University of Newfoundland in Corner Brook. From 1999 to 2003 he was Chair of Humanities. He retired from Sir Wilfred Grenfell College in 2007 with the rank of Professor of Classics and Historical Studies, and now resides in Halifax, Nova Scotia.

He considers himself to be a very eclectic composer. He is completely self-taught: the compositional skills he has have been acquired by being an avid consumer and performer of all kinds of music throughout his life. Many of his works are traditional in style while others are more avant-garde; but all of his music reflects the established traditions of the various musical periods. His music tends to be well-structured and polyphonic with unexpected elements.

He has been a prize winner in national and provincial competitions. Several of his works have been recorded on disc. In 1997, he produced a CD, "LYRE, Chamber Music for Clarinet," a recording of seven of his works for this medium. In 1999, this CD was nominated for an East Coast Music Award for Best Classical Album.

His music has been performed throughout Canada, Europe, and the United States by such organizations as the Victoria International Festival, the Holland Festival, the Toronto Symphony, the Kitchener-Waterloo Symphony, the Minneapolis Symphony, and the Newfoundland Symphony. (CMC and interview with the composer)

Chorale—Homage Anton Bruckner, Op. 39
Difficulty: Grade 5
Duration: 8:00
Composed 1989
Available through CMC (www.musiccentre.ca)

Commissioned by the Eastern Music Camp through a grant from the Newfoundland and Labrador Arts Council, *Chorale* is a tribute to Anton Bruckner (1824–1896). It received its premiere performance on August 18, 1989, at Mt. Pearl, Newfoundland, and may be heard on the recording, "To Canada, Love," by the Fredericton High School band.

Bruckner was an Austrian composer best known for his nine expansive symphonies. In his early career, he made his living as an organist and it is logical, therefore, to find that his symphonies contain many organ-like passages and melodies that resemble chorale tunes.

Parker has incorporated into this work two chorale-like melodies and some other passages from the *Symphony #4*, subtitled the Romantic, probably the best known of Bruckner's nine symphonies. It is his hope that those who perform this work will gain some appreciation of the fascinating music of this nineteenth century composer.

The work is dedicated to Paul Woodford and Gerard Walsh. (CMC and interview with the composer)

Landscapes: Opus 59, for band
Difficulty: Grade 5
Duration: 25:00
Composed 2004
Available through CMC (www.musiccentre.ca)

Landscapes was commissioned by Stemnet, a former Canadian educational organization, and the Communications Research Council of Canada through Learn Canada for the students of three high schools: J. Percy Page High School (Edmonton, Alberta), Earl of March High School (Kanata, Ontario), and Holy Heart of Mary High School (St. John's, Newfoundland and Labrador). It is dedicated to Grant Etchegary, music teacher at Holy Heart High School.

One movement was written for each school, and the entire work was to be performed over a high-speed internet connection with each movement played sequentially. Each movement (about 8 minutes long) could be performed separately, but the composer conceived of the work as a unified whole with elements of the first two movements appearing in the third.

The students in all the schools were encouraged to suggest elements that could be included in their respective movements and Parker incorporated as many as he could in the work. In the end, all of them suggested aspects of their environment, both physical and economic, and this led to his calling the work *Landscapes*. These aspects are described in greater detail in the notes for each movement. However, even though the work is firmly rooted in Canadian life, the general nature of the elements that were suggested can apply equally well to many cities and regions throughout the world: the majesty of mountains, the eternal flow of rivers, the dynamic and driving force of modern technology.

Content Notes: I. *Gateway to the North*: for the students of J. Percy Page High School (Edmonton, Alberta); II. *River of Dreams*: for the students of Earl of March High School (Kanata, Ontario); III. *Torngat*: for the students of Holy Heart of Mary High School (St. John's, Newfoundland and Labrador). (CMC and interview with the composer)

Ovation, Op. 37
Difficulty: Grade 5
Duration: 5:00
Composed 1988
Available through CMC (www.musiccentre.ca)

Ovation was commissioned by the Eastern Music Camp through a grant from the Newfoundland and Labrador Arts Council to celebrate both the 100th anniversary of the incorporation of the City of St. John's and the formal elevation of the Town of Mt. Pearl to City status. The premiere was given on August 12, 1988, at Mt. Pearl, Newfoundland.

The title of the work refers to the ovation or military parade that would be granted a victorious general by the government of ancient Rome. The general would have made a triumphant entry into the city on horseback. Parker has attempted to suggest this pagan element in the piece.

The work is in three sections. The first section contains two majestic themes, presented through fugal entries, played by the woodwinds and trumpets respectively. The middle section presents more lyrical ideas in the clarinets and saxophones. The third section builds in intensity to a featured percussion solo and fragments of the original two themes played beneath the first and last phrases of the *Ode to Newfoundland*.

Ovation is dedicated to Paul Woodford and Gerard Walsh. (CMC and interview with the composer)

Ripples
Difficulty: Grade 5
Duration: 8:00
Composed 2005
Available through CMC (www.musiccentre.ca)

Parker was asked to write a work for symphonic band to commemorate the 25th anniversary of the Herdman Collegiate Wind Symphony in Corner Brook, Newfoundland, in 2006. The work was also to serve as a musical memorial to a talented former band member, Aaron Bradbury, who died of cancer two years earlier. The title of the work was taken from one of Aaron's poems and served as the inspiration for the piece:

Ripples

Glass,
you can see your reflection.
Calm,
still.
An object touches,
ripples flow through the water.
Can you picture the years of your life?

Watch it.
Each one is a year in your life,
picture it.
It seems so precious,
watch these years fade away too.
nothing
It happens so fast,
just like life.
Cherish the small ripples,
cherish life.

Most of the work is openly celebratory, both for the 25-year existence of the Herdman Collegiate Wind Symphony and for the life of Aaron Bradbury. Towards the end, the work becomes more introspective to reflect the loss of this talented musician and human being. Here *Ripples* attempts to match the emotions and philosophy presented in Aaron's original poem.

Ripples is in the form of a passacaglia. For the passacaglia theme, Parker transliterated Aaron Bradbury's name into musical notations with a few modifications. This theme is stated boldly at the beginning in the full band and recurs throughout the work. (CMC and interview with the composer)

Terra Incognita (The Unknown Land), Op. 55
Difficulty: Grade 5
Duration: 10:00
Composed 1997
Available through CMC (www.musiccentre.ca)

Terra Incognita (The Unknown Land), Op. 55 was commissioned through a grant from the Newfoundland and Labrador Arts Council by Grant Etchegary for a tour of Newfoundland by the Avalon East Band in honor of the Cabot 500 celebrations in 1997.

The piece is a musical impression of Cabot's voyage to Newfoundland. A theme representing John Cabot (first presented by a solo clarinet) appears at the beginning and recurs throughout the work. As the piece concludes, quotes from the *Ode to Newfoundland* and the folksong *Bonavist Harbour* are heard.

The work also involves two improvised sections. In the first, the band represents the rolling waves of the ocean as Cabot's ship sails for the new world. In the second, the band depicts the ship arriving on the shores of Newfoundland: the brass blow air through their instruments to represent the waves rolling on the shore, the percussion recreates the sound of the pebbles falling back as the waves retreat, while the woodwinds represent song birds native to Newfoundland: the white throated sparrow, black-capped chickadee, song sparrow, and fox sparrow.

The work gradually builds to a climax with the Cabot theme, the *Ode to Newfoundland* and *Bonavist Harbour* uniting in a majestic finale. (CMC and interview with the composer)

MICHAEL PURVES-SMITH (B. 1945)

MICHAEL PURVES-SMITH, CONDUCTOR, COMPOSER and performer, earned a Master of Music degree from the University of British Columbia in 1971. He is currently Associate Professor of Music in the Faculty of Music at Wilfrid Laurier University, teaching both conducing and orchestration, and conducting the University's Wind Ensemble and its Baroque Ensemble. His work with these ensembles has included many important premieres, among them the first performances in North America of operas by Rameau, Lully and Gluck, and major works for wind ensemble. He is a well-known performer on baroque oboe, harpsichord, and recorder, a prolific composer and arranger, and the Artistic Director of the Wellington Winds.

Mr. Purves-Smith has written three operas, several large-scale pieces for wind ensemble, and much choral and chamber music. His works have been performed in Canada and abroad in England, the USA, France, Latvia, and Norway. His compositional philosophy calls for individual creativity in whatever musical idiom suits the project at hand. His compositions include five substantial stage works, many chamber works, choral works and compositions for wind ensemble. His most recent work, *Rimas,* a novel, 45-minute work for two flamenco dancers, small chorus, mezzo-soprano, guitar and violin, premiered on November 12, 2002 at Wilfrid Laurier University. (Wilfred Laurier University, CMC, and interview with the composer)

Chansons des Voyageurs for Wind Ensemble
Difficulty: Grade 4
Duration 11:00
Composed in 2006
Available through CMC (www.musiccentre.ca)

Voyageur is the French word for traveler. In the Fur Trade Era, it referred to a group of men employed by the various companies who acted as canoe paddlers, bundle carriers, and general laborers. Voyageurs were fond of games. They liked to play lacrosse and cat and mouse when they got the chance and, of course, to sing. The strength and endurance of the voyageurs was legendary. It was expected that each voyageur work at least 14 hours a day, paddle 55 strokes per minute and be able to carry two bundles across each portage between the lakes and rivers of the north woods. A bundle generally consisted of beaver pelts or other furs weighing about 90 lbs. on the way to Montreal, or 90 lbs. of trade goods coming from Montreal. A routine portage meant carrying 180 pounds across rugged terrain full of rocks, mud, mosquitoes and black flies.

This work was inspired by a trip to Rocky Mountain National Park in southwestern Alberta, the western terminus of the incredible journey the voyageurs made from Montreal in search of the beaver pelt. It is in three movements, each based on a song that might have been sung by the voyageurs as they paddled along the North Saskatchewan River. The movements are: 1. Rocky Mountain House (Renaud); 2. Portage la Prairie (Si j'etais petit mere); and 3. The Lakehead (Vive le roi qui n'veut pas d'moi!) (Michael Purves-Smith and The White Oak Society)

The Cremation of Sam McGee for narrator and wind ensemble with a text by Robert Service
Difficulty: Grade 5
Duration: 12:15
Composed in 2004
Available from the composer (www.michaelpurvessmith.com)

Based on the Robert Service poem about a man from the American south who can't get warm in the Yukon, this work is suitable for a Christmas performance because the story told takes place on Christmas day. Marked with mixed meter throughout, this challenging music is not for the faint hearted. The narrator must be able to read music, and the scoring for wind ensemble is designed to allow the narrator to be heard. Nevertheless, the narrator should use a microphone and a good public address system. The first performance of this work was by the Wellington Winds, Ted Fellows, narrator. (Michael Purves-Smith)

ELIZABETH RAUM (B. 1945)

ELIZABETH RAUM WAS BORN in Berlin, New Hampshire, and became a Canadian citizen in 1985. She earned her Bachelor of Music in oboe performance from the Eastman School of Music in 1966 and her Master of Music in composition from the University of Regina in 1985. In 2004 she received an honorary degree from Mount Saint Vincent in Halifax, Nova Scotia. She played principal oboe in the Atlantic Symphony Orchestra in Halifax, Nova Scotia, for 7 years before coming to Regina in 1975. She now plays principal oboe in the Regina Symphony Orchestra.

An extremely prolific composer, her works include 3 operas, over 60 chamber pieces, 15 vocal works, choral works including an oratorio, several ballets, concerti and major orchestral works. Pieces by Elizabeth Raum have won many prestigious awards, have been heard throughout North America, Europe, South America, China, Japan, and Russia, and have been broadcast extensively on the CBC. She enjoys the reputation of being one of Canada's most "accessible" composers, writing for varied mediums and in remarkably diverse styles.

Raum has written for some of the world's finest artists including Canadian soprano, Tracy Dahl; Swedish trombone virtuoso, Christian Lindberg; American tuba icon, Roger Bobo; Canadian tubist, John Griffiths; and New York Philharmonic principal hornist, Phil Meyers. She has also written for film and video, and has won awards for the scores to the documentaries "Saskatchewan River," "Like Mother, Like Daughter," and the feature length film, "Sparkle." She produced Canada's first classical video with originally written music entitled "Evolution: A Theme With Variations," which received its premiere at the CBC in 1986.

Ms. Raum has been featured in articles in the New Grove's Dictionary of Music and Musicians, the New Grove's Dictionary of Opera, the New Grove's Dictionary of Women Composers, Opera Canada, The Encyclopedia of Music in Canada, The Tuba Journal, Music Scene, and Prairie Sounds. She is also in demand as a speaker on composition and has given lectures at conferences for the Society of Composers, Authors and Music Publishers of Canada (SOCAN), Orchestras Canada, the Scotia Festival of Music, the Saskatchewan Federation of Music Teachers, the Saskatchewan Music Festival Association and the Alliance for Canadian New Music Projects. (CMC and the composer's website)

100 Years of Fanfares
Difficulty: Grade 5
Duration: 3:45
Composed in 2005
Available from the composer (www.elizabethraum.com)

100 Years of Fanfares was commsissioned by the Saskatchewan Band Association to celebrate the 100th anniversary of Saskatchewan's confederation with

Canada. The National Youth Band of Canada, for whom it was written, premiered it in May 2005, with Marvin Eckroth conducting.

Fanfares have been part of wind music since before biblical times, and the trumpet holds a special place in pageants and ceremonies both military and civic. This work uses fanfares and "echoes of fanfares" to represent Saskatchewan's past century. The opening fanfare (the present) in A minor is bold and forthright, followed by a maestoso in which the music is played by woodwinds and muted brass as if at a distance (the past). Almost all the brass join together to mark the return to the present as they repeat the trumpet theme in the opening fanfare. The original key of A minor gives way to F Major as the work reaches a satisfying, fortissimo conclusion. (CMC, Jennifer McAllister, Encyclopedia of Music in Canada, and interview with the composer)

Sodbuster
Difficulty: Grade 3
Duration: 5:00
Composed in 1999
Available through CMC (www.musiccentre.ca) and from the composer
    (www.elizabethraum.com)

The term "sodbuster" refers to one who breaks the sod. That was the name given to the early pioneers who came to Saskatchewan 100 years ago to settle and farm. They cut squares out of the sod, the grassy top layer of soil, stacked them to make the four walls of their tiny one room houses, and then topped them with wooden roofs. Then they farmed the land and formed communities.

When Ms. Raum was asked to write a new work for the Saskatchewan Band Association, they wanted something exciting and optimistic, something that would reflect the personality of the people of Saskatchewan. In response to that desire she wrote a combination march and overture, full of fanfare and melody. (CMC and interview with the composer)

GODFREY RIDOUT (1918–1984)

GODFREY RIDOUT'S INTEREST IN music was kindled early by being taken to concerts of the newly reformed Toronto Symphony Orchestra. He received his musical education in Toronto under Ettore Mazzoleni, Charles Peaker and Healey Willan. He was appointed to the staff of the Toronto Conservatory of Music (now the Royal Conservatory) in 1939 and to the Faculty of Music, University of Toronto, in 1948 where he was an Associate Professor. He retired from the University's Faculty of Music in 1982. He was also music director of the Eaton Operatic Society from 1949 to 1958, and worked for a number of Canadian music publications, including *Canadian Music* and the *Canadian Review of Music and Art.*

Often described as old-fashioned in his musical tastes, Ridout achieved his first musical success in 1938 with *Ballade for Viola and String Orchestra.* He enjoyed popular music, and composed many drama scores for Canadian Broadcasting Corporation Radio and film scores for the National Film Board early in his career.

Moved by the formation of the State of Israel, he wrote *Esther,* a dramatic symphony that critics lauded. He won further acclaim in 1953 with *Holy Sonnets* and in 1959 with *Music for a Young Prince,* dedicated to Prince Charles. His list of music is long and encompasses almost every musical form.

Ridout is properly characterized as a conservative traditionalist. His view of musical literature was, if not narrow, certainly selective, but students can testify that the works he admired he knew thoroughly. He had an unusually well cultivated sense of English language expression, and his manner was a quietly correct one. But counterbalancing his adherence to traditional values were, in his teaching, a liberalist's tolerance for ideas presented in open discussion, and, in his personality and his creative work, often an irrepressible boyishness and sense of fun. In his view there not only was room for deep sentiment and mysticism in his music but also for the sheer fun of "tootling on your piccolo." (CMC, The Canadian Encyclopedia, and The National Archives of Canada)

Partita Accademica
Difficulty: Grade 3
Duration: 9:35
Published 1985 by G.V. Thompson
Available through CMC (www.musiccentre.ca)

This 1969 tonal work is written in traditional style, and was premiered by the University of Toronto Concert Band on March 22, 1970. The four movements are: *1. Flourish of Fond Farewell; 2. March; 3. Noctourne;* and *4. Scherzo.* The flourish is dedicated to Arnold Walter, president of the Canadian Music Centre; and the March to Robert A. Rosevear, founding conductor of the University of Toronto Concert Band.

Partita Accademica opens with a brass fanfare followed by an Elgarian march, the trio of which is derived from the inversion of the work's opening material. The *Noctourne* that follows is quiet, featuring solo instruments in a lyrical style. The final *Scherzo* is based on quasi-folk materials that jump from one instrumental section to another, making a lively and colorful closing to the suite. The march has the proper maestoso quality to warrant being performed alone on ceremonial occasions. (CMC and Timothy Maloney)

Tafelmusik
Difficulty: Grade 4
Duration: 7:00
Composed in 1976
Available through CMC (www.musiccentre.ca)

Commissioned by the Alumni Association of the Faculty of Music, University of Toronto, *Tafelmusik* is scored for 16 winds, essentially a small orchestral wind section. Its jazzy style and title (Table Music) suggest that it was intended for performance during a banquet. Its premiere was just such a setting, in honor of Robert Rosevear's 30th anniversary fete as Professor of Music Education at the University of Toronto. It would be an excellent work to contrast with the more serious pieces that might occupy a concert program. While *Tafelmusik* is intended to be performed in its entirety, each of the two movements is strong enough to be performed separately.

The two movements are entitled *Blues* and *Finale.* The first movement, in ABA form, is sultry and languid with a walking bass line and solos by trumpet and clarinet. The second movement is a brilliant allegro reminiscent of the closing act of a drama. Lively and cheerful, it opens with a fanfare and presents several different motifs that might denote a set of characters. All the motifs are joined in counterpoint to produce a rousing conclusion. (CMC, Keith Kinder, and Timothy Maloney)

A pedagogical discussion of this work can be found on page 63 of *Guidelist of Unpublished Canadian Band Music Suitable for Student Performers* by Patricia Martin Shand.

SID ROBINOVITCH (B. 1942)

A NATIVE OF MANITOBA, Sid Robinovitch received his Doctorate in Communications from the University of Illinois and taught social sciences at York University in Toronto. Since 1977 he has devoted himself to musical composition, having studied at Indiana University and at the Royal Conservatory of Toronto with Samuel Dolin. He presently lives in Winnipeg, Canada, where he works as a composer and teacher.

Having written for a wide variety of musical media, Robinovitch has received commissions from performers such as the Elmer Iseler Singers, the Canadian Piano Trio and the Winnipeg Symphony Orchestra. His works have been broadcast frequently on CBC radio, including original pieces based on folk-tales from around the world and arrangements of Judeo-Spanish folk songs. In 1990 his *Sons of Jacob* for violin and piano was nominated for a JUNO award as best classical composition, and in 1991 his *Adieu Babylon* was the commissioned work at the Eckhardt-Gramatté National Music Competition.

While many of Robinovitch's works are rooted in traditional or folk material, they often have a distinctly contemporary flavor as well. *Dreaming Lolita*, for example, is a dramatic retelling in poetic form of the famous Nabokov novel, and in *Psalms of Experience* the choral textures are infused with elements of Balinese music and rhythmic chanting. In addition to his concert works, Robinovitch has written music for film, radio and TV, where he is probably best known for his theme for CBC-TV's satirical comedy series, "The Newsroom."

Klezmer Suite, a recording devoted entirely to his music performed by the Winnipeg Symphony under the direction of Bramwell Tovey, was nominated for a 2002 JUNO award and received a Prairie Music Award for outstanding classical recording. (CMC)

Sphinx
Difficulty: Grade 3
Duration: 8:29
Published in 1995
Available through CMC (www.musiccentre.ca) and Comprint
   (www3.sympatico.ca/comprint)

Sphinx was commissioned by Jeff Kula for the John Henderson Junior High Wind Ensemble in Winnipeg, Manitoba. The poem that inspired the music, "Sphinx" by Deborah Chandra (below), resulted in a very accessible and descriptive work that includes solos for trombones and woodwinds. It is very modern and very mysterious.

Sphinx

As the sun
Is going down, And shadows mix
With yellow sand,
He rises slowly,
Stretches, stands,
Wades into the Nile to wash
Mummy-dust and sand fleas off –
Licks heavy paws
With heavy tongue
Until the cool night air is gone.
While on Egyptian earth
He drops dry purrs.
Ground out like powdered rock.

(CMC and interview with the composer)

West of Bali
Difficulty: Grade 4
Duration: 7:58
Composed in 1996
Available through CMC (www.musiccentre.ca)

Winnipeg composer Sid Robinovitch has a strong interest in world music. As the title of this work implies, he has integrated Balinese elements with Latin rhythms to create *West of Bali*. The scoring is for standard concert band plus piano, electric bass, and a large percussion complement. The work is based on the third movement of a choral work by the composer entitled *Psalms of Experience.*

West of Bali opens with two simultaneous, repetitive melodic figures that are later introduced at half speed in trumpet and saxophone, then at half speed again in horns and euphonium. The repetitive, gamelan-like figuration in the flutes and piano accounts for the "Balinese" reference in the title, while the Latin rhythms that appear later in the piece, played by the electric bass and percussion, give the music a distinctly "Western" flavor as well. Combining the two figurations creates the East/West amalgam. The various sections are connected by a chorale that appears three times in the course of the work. *West of Bali* is an excellent introduction to Canadian wind band music that draws on other cultures. (CMC, Keith Kinder, and interview with the composer)

NICOLE RODRIGUE (B. 1943)

NICOLE RODRIGUE STUDIED AT the École de Musique Vincent d'Indy where she was awarded her bachelor's degree and a specialist teaching certificate. She continued her training at the Faculty of Music of the University of Montreal and received a license in secular music. Feeling a growing attraction for composition, she went to McGill University where she joined in the composition class of professors Istvan Anhalt and Alcides Lanza, and became the first woman to receive a Master of Musical Arts (MMA) in composition. Her broad experience in education led her toward research focusing on an inventive environment in teaching music, and she enrolled at the University of Montreal in the Ph.D. program in education. She experimented with the "Music Mouse Pro" creative software of the American composer Laurie Spiegel, and she wrote a guide in pedagogical activities. From 1970 to 1998, she taught at the School Commission of Montreal. Her musical activities include her first European studies with the Jeunesses Musicales of Belgium and later, in Darmstadt where her work *Nasca* was given its world premiere. Her compositions include works for solo, duet, band, chamber music and choral music. (CMC)

Désastre
Difficulty: Grade 5
Duration: 5:00
Composed in 1977
Available through CMC (www.musiccentre.ca)

Stylistically contemporary, this piece is graphically notated, with time indicated in seconds. Explanatory notes and instructions to aid the conductor and performers are provided in French. Performers have considerable freedom in interpreting the graphic notation, which contains no traditional rhythm, melody, or harmony. Because there is no conventional rhythmic notation and no use of the accent structure inherent in the usual 4/4 pattern, the players must seek an overall sense of musical form and dramatic shaping. The main interest lies in changing textures and timbres. An expressive improvised trombone solo is featured. The piece builds to a fortissimo climax, then disappears with the sound of a candle being blown out. This work provides opportunities to explore graphic notation and a variety of instrumental timbres. (Patricia Shand)

A pedagogical discussion of this work can be found on page 64 of *Guidelist of Unpublished Canadian Band Music Suitable for Student Performers* by Patricia Martin Shand.

RONALD ROYER (B. 1959)

BORN IN LOS ANGELES into a family of professional musicians, Ronald Royer began his career as a cellist, performing with such ensembles as the Utah Symphony, Pacific Symphony and Toronto Symphony, as well as working in the Motion Picture and Television Industry in Los Angeles.

Since obtaining a Masters Degree in Composition from the University of Toronto Mr. Royer is quickly emerging as a prominent composer with numerous commissions, performances and commercial recordings. His compositions encompass a variety of ensembles including orchestral, choral, wind ensembles and chamber groups. His music employs expressive melodies, rich harmonies, energetic rhythms, colorful orchestrations and tight and integrated structures. Los Angeles music producer and musicologist Jeannie Pool writes, "A musician's composer, Ronald Royer's music is beautifully conceived, well-structured and intricately detailed. His musical sensibility, dramatic flair, and clear headedness result in new music which is a joy to listeners and players alike."

He is also in demand as a conductor, lecturer, concert host and musical adviser. From 1998 to 2002, Mr. Royer served as Composer-in-Residence for the Toronto Sinfonietta, for which he wrote six orchestra commissions. In June 2004, he became the Composer-in-Residence for the Mississauga Symphonic Association, supported by a residency grant from the Canada Council for the Arts. This residency has included developing an educational outreach program called *The Hollywood Sound*. Mr. Royer also received a Eureka! Centre grant to develop curriculum materials for this project. He currently serves as composer-in-residence for Orchestras Mississauga, supported by a residency grant from the Canada Council for the Arts, while also teaching at University of Toronto Schools (UTS). Mr. Royer is a member of the Society of Composers, Authors and Music Publishers of Canada (SOCAN)/ASCAP and is an associate composer of the Canadian Music Centre. (© Eighth Note Publications, used by permission)

Overture to an Unscripted Movie
Difficulty: Grade 4
Duration: 12:00
Published 2004 by Eighth Note Publications (www.enpmusic.com)

Overture to An Unscripted Movie was composed to pay homage to the orchestral scores written for Hollywood action/adventure films. The Overture is in four sections: *The Hero, The Villain, The Love Theme, and The Fight.* Since the Overture was written for an unscripted movie, the composer encourages both performers and audience members to create their own movie plots. The work requires a strong pianist and low woodwinds for best effect.

To write this composition, Mr. Royer drew on his extensive work as a freelance cellist in the Motion Picture and Television industry in Los Angeles in the

1980's. Some of the films he worked on are: Star Trek 3 and 4, Lethal Weapon, Footloose, Gremlins, The Outsiders, Children of a Lesser God, and television shows such as Little House on the Prairie, Dallas, and Fantasy Island. He also performed under many of the top film composers, including Jerry Goldsmith, Michael Kamen, Henry Mancini, Lalo Schifrin and John Williams. (Orchestras Mississauga and Eighth Note Publications, used by permission)

JEFFREY RYAN (B. 1962)

JEFFREY RYAN WAS RAISED in Fergus, Ontario. He fled the School of Business and Economics at Wilfrid Laurier University to join the Faculty of Music, from which he graduated in 1984 with an Honors Bachelor of Music degree and the gold medal in music. After earning a Master's degree in composition from the University of Toronto, he went on to receive his Doctor of Musical Arts degree in music composition from The Cleveland Institute of Music in 1995, where he studied with Donald Erb. Previous teachers include Alexina Louie, Lothar Klein, Mariano Etkin, Boyd McDonald, and Owen Underhill. He is an Associate Composer with the Canadian Music Centre, and a member of the Canadian League of Composers.

Mr. Ryan's varied catalogue includes opera, art song, choral music, chamber ensemble and orchestral works, and his compositions have been performed and broadcast across Canada and internationally. He currently serves as composer-in-residence with the Vancouver Symphony Orchestra, and as composer advisor for the chamber music presenter Music TORONTO. Previously, he served for two seasons as an affiliate composer with the Toronto Symphony, has been a featured guest composer in the "Soundstreams—Canada's Encounters" series in Toronto, and has served as visiting guest composer with the Winnipeg Symphony New Music Festival, Tapestry New Opera (Toronto), Brandon New Music (Manitoba), the Strings of the Future Festival in Ottawa, and the Bowling Green (Ohio) State University's New Music and Art Festival. He has also held residencies with the Windsor Symphony as The SOCAN Foundation's Composer in the Community. (CMC and the composer's website, www.jeffreyryan .com)

Orillia Panorama
Difficulty: Grade 3
Duration: 10:30
Composed in 1999
Available through CMC (www.musiccentre.ca)

This work was commissioned by the Orillia Wind Ensemble through the Ontario Arts Council. Its premiere was given on May 2, 1999, at the Orillia Opera House, Orillia, Ontario; Orillia Wind Ensemble, Roy Menagh, conductor. The work contains four movements: *I. Laclie (Cross-Country); II. Brant (Colour and Stillness); III. Canice (Water Music); IV. Tecumseth (Industrial Revolution).*

The composer writes, "The four movements of *Orillia Panorama* find their inspiration in the city and surroundings of Orillia, Ontario. I am always fascinated by the history of places, and as I delved into the history of Orillia, I was intrigued by the development of the early market square and its subsequent move a little farther south, to what would eventually become the city center.

I imagined what it might be like to take myself back in time, to stand in that original market square and then to see the city and countryside develop and grow around me as the years pass into the present.

"The four streets that bordered the first market square provide the titles for these four short character pieces. From the middle of that square and looking to *Laclie*, to the west, we see the rolling countryside now so popular in the winter with skiers. *Brant*, to the north, looks out upon the peaceful vista and beautiful fall colors of cottage country. Turning to the east, *Canice* faces the waters of Lake Couchiching, sparkling in the summer sunlight. Finally, *Tecumseth* looks to the south, where the city's industry sprang forth, most notably in the area of car manufacture, and now the direction of many a morning commute." (CMC and the composer's website, www.jeffreyryan.com)

THOMAS SCHUDEL (B. 1937)

THOMAS SCHUDEL WAS, UNTIL his retirement in 2003, professor of music at the University of Regina in Regina, Saskatchewan, Canada, where he taught composition, harmony, counterpoint and analysis classes. Born in Defiance, Ohio, he moved to Canada in 1964 and became a Canadian citizen in 1974. He studied composition at Ohio State University with Dr. Marshall Barnes where he received his bachelor's and master's degrees. He earned his DMA at the University of Michigan where he studied composition with Prof. Ross Lee Finney and Dr. Leslie Basset.

His *Symphony No. 1* won First Prize in the City of Trieste's International Competition for Orchestral Composition in 1972 and was premiered there that year. Commissions have come from The Canada Council, Saskatchewan Arts Board, The Regina Symphony Orchestra, The Canadian Broadcasting Corporation, The Saskatchewan Music Educators Association, The Saskatchewan Choral Federation, The Saskatchewan Music Festival Association, The Saskatoon Saxophone Quartet, The Regina Saxophone Quartet, and The University of Regina Chamber Singers. His works have been performed across Canada, in the United States, Italy and Ireland.

His compositions until the early 1980s often used a modified twelve-tone structure with a great deal of instrumental color. They were polytonal, developing structurally from small motivic cells. His music since then is often modal and tonal but still with a considerable amount of chromaticism.

Many of his works are published in the United States and Canada. He is an associate composer of the Canadian Music Centre, and the performing rights organization, SOCAN. (CMC and the Canadian Encyclopedia)

Elegy and Exaltation
Difficulty: Grade 5
Duration: 7:00
Composed in 1984
Available through CMC (www.musiccentre.ca)

Elegy and Exaltation was commissioned by the University of Saskatchewan for the University of Saskatchewan Wind Ensemble. This challenging work is suitable for university and professional ensembles. It is based on twelve-tone principles but with a tonal basis. (CMC and interview with the composer)

Triptych
Difficulty: Grade 6
Duration: 20:00
Composed in 1978
Published 1991 by Seesaw Music
Available through CMC (www.musiccentre.ca)

This work was commissioned by the Canadian Broadcasting Corporation for the CBC Saskatchewan Festival, 1978, and is dedicated to a friend of the composer who passed away. *Triptych* consists of four movements: *I. Adagio, allegro, andante; II. Vivace, largo, vivace; III. Andante ma non troppo, allegro con fuoco, adagio.* (CMC and interview with the composer)

NORMAN SHERMAN (B. 1924)

THE MOST DISTINCTIVE CHARACTERISTICS of Norman Sherman's compositional process are his meticulous concern for craftsmanship and constant attention to detail, combined with an excellent command of orchestration and an individual style free of any strong outside influences. His sensitive feeling for the orchestra is the result of his having been a first chair player in symphony orchestras for many years.

Born, raised and schooled in Boston, Sherman graduated from Boston University with a degree in composition while also studying bassoon with Ernst Panenka and chamber music performance with Fernand Gillet, both of the Boston Symphony Orchestra. During that period he had three years of intensive studies in advanced compositional techniques with Dr. R. Brogue Henning of Harvard University. While attending Tanglewood he met Olivier Messiaen, with whom he subsequently studied Musical Aesthetics and Analysis at the Conservatoire National de Paris.

Arriving in Canada in 1957 to take up the position of principal bassoon with the Winnipeg Symphony Orchestra and the CBC Orchestra, Sherman was active both as a composer for CBC radio drama and as a conductor/arranger of light music for his own radio shows. After four years in Winnipeg, Norman Sherman left Canada to accept the principal bassoon position with The Hague Philharmonic Orchestra (Het Residentie-Orkest) of The Netherlands, where he remained for many years.

Returning to Canada in 1975, (Sherman holds both American and Canadian citizenship) he was appointed to the position of Senior Instructor in composition and orchestration in the School of Music of Queen's University, Kingston, and remained in that position until 1999, when he decided to stop teaching in order to devote all his energies to compositional activities. At present he resides in London, Ontario.

All of Norman Sherman's manuscripts and work papers have been accepted into the archives of the music section of the National Library of Canada, Ottawa, and many of his compositions are found in the libraries of universities and music schools in the United States, Canada, Finland and Denmark. He is a member of the Canadian League of Composers, an associate member of the Canadian Music Centre and an affiliate of the Society of Composers, Authors and Music Publishers of Canada (SOCAN). (CMC and The Canadian Encyclopedia)

The Pioneers: suite for band
Difficulty: Grade 4
Duration: 15:00
Composed in 1983
Available through CMC (www.musiccentre.ca)

The composer writes, "This composition was commissioned by the Canadian Armed Forces Vimy Band of Kingston, Ontario through the Ontario Arts Council. The commanding officer and conductor of the band asked me to compose a piece of music that would be, as he termed, 'audience friendly'. To fulfill his request I tried to think of music with a sort of program to which the audience could relate. And so I decided to compose a band composition in three movements and gave a title to each movement that would create the atmosphere of a story and stir the listener's mind. Therefore the three movements have the following titles: *1. Wagon Trains; 2. New Towns* and *3. Celebrations.*

The premiere performance took place in London, Ontario in 1984. The band performed it a year later in Kingston, Ontario. It has been also performed by the United States Air Force "Heartland of America Band" throughout their area in the midwest and has been recorded by that same band on their CD entitled "Heartland Journeys." (Interview with the composer)

JACK SIRULNIKOFF (B. 1931)

JACK SIRULNIKOFF STUDIED COMPOSITION with, among others, Istvan Anhalt, Henry Brant and John Weinzweig, and received a Bachelor of Music (composition) degree from McGill University in 1956. He acquired a Teaching Fellowship at Bennington College in Vermont in 1958 in a program that led to a Master of Arts degree in Music Composition. He has taught instrumental music and English in Ontario, and classroom music at the Nova Scotia Teachers College in Truro, Nova Scotia. As a composer, he provided music for the National Film Board and arranged music for the CBC. His works may be divided into three categories: light music, music for amateur performers, and music utilizing serial methods and dodecaphony. He has experimented with jazz, electronic music, and the use of computers in performance.

He is now retired, but keeps busy mainly with computers and music. (CMC and the composer's website)

Nova Scotia Fantasy
Difficulty: Grade 3
Duration: 7:00
Composed in 1967
Available through CMC (www.musiccentre.ca)

The piece was written in Canada's Centennial Year for the Truro, Nova Scotia Concert Band, and is based on four Nova Scotia folksongs, as collected by the well-known folklorist, Helen Creighton. The introduction is based on *Sally Round the Corner, O,* and serves to set the seagoing mood. This is followed by *The Nova Scotia Song,* a very famous and popular song in the Maritimes. This exquisite Aeolian tune is virtually the provincial anthem and is much loved outside the province as well. Its history is obscure, but it probably was adapted from an old British sailing song. It features a trumpet solo as well as a somewhat tricky rhythmic background. This is followed by two verses of *Captain Conrod,* a humorous piece whose first line begins, "Come all you bold fellows that follows the sea," and which provides a change of tempo and meter. It also features some mild dissonance. The second verse is a striking variation based on augmentation of the individual notes of the melody. A gentle Acadian fiddle tune brings the work back to *Farewell to Nova Scotia,* which ends the piece in a grandiose flourish. Intended for younger bands, this work maintains interest through appealing, contrasted melodies and effective compositional technique. (CMC and Keith Kinder)

A pedagogical discussion of this work can be found on page 29 of *Guidelist of Unpublished Canadian Band Music Suitable for Student Performers* by Patricia Martin Shand.

Variations on a Rollicking Tune
Difficulty: Grade 3
Duration: 3:35
Composed in 1977
Available through CMC and Counterpoint Musical Services
(www.counterpointmusic.ca)

Jack Sirulnikoff's lighthearted *Variations on a Rollicking Tune* is based on the flamboyant dance tune, *I's the B'y That Builds the Boat,* one of the best known of all Newfoundland folk songs. The song has dozens of verses. Since the words are chosen for sound rather than meaning, most of the text makes little sense, although some phrases are instructions to dancers. In Newfoundland, singers at dances are expected to make up their own verses to this melody, many of which are crude or bawdy.

In his *Variations,* Sirulnikoff picked up on the irreverent nature of the song and made his arrangement into a fine example of musical humor by featuring a solo woodblock in the introduction, creating abrupt changes of texture and incorporating amusing twists in the surface rhythm. The variations incorporate primarily changes of meter, but also make use of ornamentation and solo textures contrasted with full band. In variation one, the tune is stated in brief motives tossed around the band, resulting in uneven phrase lengths. Solo textures and impressive contrary motion counterpoint are also featured. The second variation is a quick waltz, while the third is a duple meter march with the melody heavily ornamented. Variation four combines the march with the original triple meter tune. A da capo al coda brings the work to a rousing conclusion. This delightful work, intended for younger bands, is robust and exciting, and successfully captures the exuberance associated with this folk song. It is quite popular in Canada, and has been performed often. It was first performed in 1977 at the Midwest Band Clinic in Chicago. (CMC and Keith Kinder)

A recording of this work is available on the CD "North Winds—Canadian Wind Band Music," which may be ordered from the University of Manitoba, Faculty of Music, 65 Dafoe Road, Winnipeg, Manitoba, Canada R3T 2N2 or by calling (204) 474-9310. A recording of this work also is available on the CD "A Lakeshore Concert," by the Lakeshore Concert Band of Montreal, and may be ordered by emailing the band at *lakeshoreconcertband@coolgoose.com.*

Anita Sleeman (b. 1930)

Anita Sleeman was born in San Jose, California to immigrant parents. She grew up in a rich multi-cultural area in San Francisco. Her father, Alexander Andrés, was a graphic artist and painter, and her mother, an art student and milliner, hailed from Stavropol in the Caucasus region of Russia. Exhibiting a high aptitude for music at a very young age, she began piano lessons at age three, adding trumpet and horn during her school years. Sleeman's first major composition, a processional march for band, was played at her community college graduation.

After attending Placer College in California she and her family emigrated to the remote Bella Coola region of British Columbia, Canada. Sleeman taught music appreciation, ear training, and band to the children at the local one-room school, five of the students being her own children.

Following a move to the Vancouver area of B.C., Sleeman attended the University of British Columbia, where she studied with Jean Coulthard and Cortland Hultberg, earning a Bachelor of Music degree in 1967. That same year she and four other founding members formed the Delta Youth Orchestra, which remains a training program for young musicians in the Vancouver area. While continuing her studies at UBC she obtained a Graduate Fellowship and taught in the Electronic Music Studio. She earned her Master of Music degree in 1974. Sleeman was a member of the Music Faculty at Capilano College for a number of years before she returned to California to attend graduate school at the University of Southern California in Los Angeles. Here she studied composition with Frederick Lesemann, composition and orchestration with James Hopkins, and contemporary conducting and composition with Earle Brown, and received her Doctorate in 1982. During this time she also studied at the Dick Grove Jazz School in Los Angeles.

At an early age Sleeman was introduced to the music of Olivier Messiaen, whose inspiration has been important in her development. Other influences on Sleeman's music are Varèse, Stravinsky, Koechlin, Lígeti and Bartok. Her eclectic style has also been colored by her own ethnic background and her interest in jazz. She greatly admires the work of the late Frank Zappa, to whose memory she has dedicated performances of her own pieces. The grandmother of 12, and great-grandmother of 4, Sleeman now lives in West Vancouver, British Columbia, where she conducts the Ambleside Orchestra, and composes at her home studio. (CMC and interview with the composer)

Bourée Variations (on the French folk song *Au Bois de ma Tante*)
Difficulty: Grade 4
Duration: 4:15
Composed in 1972
Available through the composer (aragonmusic@yahoo.com)

The composer studied ethnomusicology at the University of British Columbia, and this set of variations is the result of an ethnomusicological survey of French folk songs. It received its premiere in 1972 at the University of British Columbia, under the direction of Paul Douglas. The French folk song *Au Bois de ma Tante (In the Woods of my Aunt)* is referred to by ethnomusicologists as a "sung bourée." As in the French language, there are few strong accents, and the theoretical downbeat becomes vague. The composer has chosen to use various rhythmic devices such as hemiola, polyrhythms, etc., and only occasionally exploit the Baroque concept of the prominent upbeat in the bourée. (Interview with the composer)

Cantus
Difficulty: Grade 5
Duration: 7:00
Composed in 1981
Available through the composer (aragonmusic@yahoo.com)

"Cantus" refers to a chant-like theme developed throughout the piece. Its premiere was with the University of Southern California Composers' Ensemble, Joyce Shintani, conductor. The theme appears at the very beginning, with three horns playing in unison; however, one is open, one stopped and one muted. After various permutations, the theme is heard in its entirety in the baritone, and later in the alto saxophone. A solo flute trails away at the end. (Interview with the composer)

Carol of the Bells: A Fantasy on the Christmas Carol
Difficulty: Grade 4
Duration: 3:00
Composed in 1989
Available through the composer (aragonmusic@yahoo.com) and
    CMC (www.musiccentre.ca)

The premiere of *Carol of the Bells* took place on December 12, 1989, at the South Delta High School Auditorium, Tsawwassen, B.C.; the Delta Band, Rob Colquhoun, conducting. Based on one of the composer's favorite carols, the first half of the piece is a straightforward version. The second half explores variations on fragments of the theme, beginning with a cantabile horn. When the main theme returns, the rhythms are altered. The bass clarinet, glockenspiel and tubular chimes are featured prominently. (Interview with the composer)

Celebration Overture
Difficulty: Grade 5
Duration: 6:00
Composed in 1994
Available through the composer (aragonmusic@yahoo.com)
    and CMC (www.musiccentre.ca)

This overture begins and ends with fanfares; these were extracted from the final movement of Sleeman's *Quintet for Brass*, and expanded in this work. The main body of the piece is made up of variations on theme fragments taken from the fanfare. These include march-like structures, a fugato, and a rubato/cantabile section. The piece was commissioned by the West Vancouver Concert Band for its 25th anniversary celebration, and received its premiere by that ensemble in November 1994 at the Mt. Seymour United Church, North Vancouver, BC, Arthur Smith, conductor. (Interview with the composer)

Cryptic Variations
Difficulty: Grade 6
Duration: ca. 8:00
Composed in 2000
Available through the composer (aragonmusic@yahoo.com) and
    CMC (www.musiccentre.ca)

Cryptic Variations is based on a complex numerical and serial sequence. It was commissioned by Vancouver Community College for the 25th anniversary of its King Edward Campus. The premiere, on March 18, 2000, at the Caulfield School Auditorium in West Vancouver, BC, was performed by the Vancouver Community College Wind Ensemble, Jerry Lloyd Domer, conductor.

The college's wind ensemble also served as a community band, and there the composer played principal horn for some years. She is fond of cryptic crossword puzzles—those which go beyond ordinary definitions, and anagram or hide clues, chop up words, use off-the-wall references, slang, abbreviations, etc. Sleeman did just that to the music, fragmenting, serializing in all its aspects, minimalizing, using numerical sequences, and generally being tricky. The slow center section features alto flute (an alternative alto sax part is provided), and multiple percussionists are featured throughout. (Interview with the composer)

Quetzalcoatl
Difficulty: Grade 5
Duration: 11:00
Composed: 1973
Available through the composer (aragonmusic@yahoo.com)

The University of British Columbia Wind Ensemble, David Berger, director, premiered this vigorous one-movement work in 1973. The composer was fascinated by the image of a feathered serpent. This music reflects those images, but in no way attempts to be an accurate portrayal of the legend. It was written for a very large ensemble—there were 14 flutists in the premiere performance—and includes such rare instruments as contrabass clarinet. It is written in one movement with definite sections. The *Temple of the Moon* sets the mood, with multiple filigree patterns on a pentatonic motif in the upper registers, plus some chordal figures. *Invocation* is a short interlude, featuring horns in several registers. *Sacrificial March* represents the "chosen ones" in a procession to the altar. The second short interlude, *Lament,* leads into *Dance of the Feathered Serpent,* a short but rambunctious, multi-rhythmic movement. (Interview with the composer)

JEFF SMALLMAN (B. 1965)

JEFF SMALLMAN WAS BORN in Brantford, Ontario. At the age of eight, he began piano lessons and began writing music soon after. He attended the University of Western Ontario and, in 1987, graduated with an honors degree in Theory and Composition. While at Western, he studied with Alan Heard and Gerhard Wuensch, and found many different influences from as early as the Medieval period. Various 20th century techniques, including serialism, aleatoric, 12-tone, etc., failed to attract Mr. Smallman, whose melodic talents incorporate a blend of Baroque, Classical, Romantic, and Impressionist styles.

He has written for a wide variety of ensembles, ranging from solo instruments to full orchestra, covering a range of styles and difficulty levels. This variety of styles has led people to compare his music to such composers as Bach, Ravel, Debussy, Mahler, Poulenc, Ibert, and Shostakovich.

In 1991 he was a finalist in the Search for New Music competition hosted by the Canadian Band Association. The work he submitted was his concert band piece *Spirit of Adventure*.

Smallman has received many commissions for new works. The numerous pieces he has written for schools, churches and individuals include works for concert band, solo flute, clarinet choir, saxophone quartet and over 20 pieces for various size choirs. His trumpet sextet *Fanfare for Prince Henry* was written for and accepted by the Prince and Princess of Wales in 1984.

Performances of Mr. Smallman's compositions have been given throughout Canada, the United States, China and Hungary. Two of Mr. Smallman's choral works, *Brier* and *Sentinels of Glory*, were declared competition winners in 2004. Subsequent to these wins, Mr. Smallman was admitted to the Canadian League of Composers. (Eighth Note Publications, used by permission, and Lighthouse Music Publications, used by permission)

And Birds Will Sing Again
Difficulty: Grade 2
Duration: 3:00
Published 2000 by Eighth Note Publications (www.enpmusic.com)

This lyric tune is taken from a musical entitled *All's Fair*, written by the composer. Set during the Second World War, this song is sung in memory of friends and family who have been lost in battle. Flutes and bells, and later the baritone, play the melody during the verses while the trumpets are given the melody during the refrains. This piece for younger bands begins quietly, builds slowly through to the end of the second chorus, then quietly winds its way through the last phrase. (© Eighth Note Publications, used by permission)

Arkhangelsk
Difficulty: Grade 4
Duration: 6:30
Published 2003 by Lighthouse Music
  (www.lighthousemusicpublications.com)

Arkhangelsk, formerly called Archangel in English, is a city in the far north of European Russia, and was the chief seaport of medieval Russia. This work was commissioned by the Parry Sound High School Wind Ensemble, M. Keddy, Director. Low brass and timpani immediately set the tone of the piece as they present the driving opening theme. This theme is picked up by the woodwinds and moves into a more martial section where the trumpets are given the melody. The ensemble then moves into a slower, plaintive folksong-like section, where the alto saxophone is given a solo melody to play over a droning bass ostinato. In this very lyric section, melody is passed among the various instrument groups freely. At the conclusion of this middle section, the mood is brought back to the opening martial theme, which builds to a fever pitch only to have the alto saxophone intrude with its solo melody for two measures before the ensemble overpowers it with two concluding chords. Mirroring its origins, it is very Russian in flavor. (Interview with the composer)

Coming Home
Difficulty: Grade 1
Duration: 2:20
Published 1998 by Eighth Note Publications (www.enpmusic.com)

This grade 1 work is characterized by interesting and musical parts for young musicians. The bass line combined with interesting melodic material make this an excellent work for young band. The engaging melody and enjoyable background can be learned in a short period of time. (© Eighth Note Publications, used by permission)

Grand Procession
Difficulty: Grade 3
Duration: 3:20
Published 1998 by Eighth Note Publications (www.enpmusic.com)

Originally written as a wedding march for solo organ, this piece has adeptly been expanded for the concert band. Fanfares in the brass provide interesting contrast to the stately, lyric themes within, and the melodies are passed off between instruments and sections for variety and interest. (© Eighth Note Publications, used by permission)

Sinfonietta
Difficulty: Grade 5
Duration: 16:00
Published 2003 by Lighthouse Music
    (www.lighthousemusicpublications.com)

Sinfonietta was commissioned by the Stratford Concert Band in memory of euphonium soloist John Belland, and is written in three movements. Movement #1 begins with a fanfare reminiscent in tone of Mussorgsky. This gives way to a restless, repetitive figure with a slight Spanish flavor. The second movement begins and ends with a euphonium solo, and is very lyrical throughout. The third movement, which begins with four sharp chords, constantly drives forward and employs constant changes in texture. Skilled band writing takes full advantage of the tone colors available in a wind ensemble. (Interview with the composer)

Shades of Majesty
Difficulty: Grade 3
Duration: 5:20
Published 2005 by Lighthouse Music
    (www.lighthousemusicpublications.com)

Shades of Majesty was commissioned by the London Concert Band, Robert Kennedy conductor, with assistance from the London Arts Council. Written as a work to honor former conductors Martin Boundy and Frank Barrett, this work begins and ends with energy. A series of staccato chords leads to a frenzied line in the flute section accompanied by repeated chords in the French horns. Meter changes and lively melody provide a festive atmosphere. The middle section melody is given to the French horns in a chorale reminiscent of Wagner or Strauss. A moment of discord gives way to a recap of the opening section. (Interview with the composer)

Pavana Antiqua
Difficulty: Grade 2
Duration: 2:15
Published 1998 by Eighth Note Publications (www.enpmusic.com)

A *pavane* was a court dance from the 16th or 17th century. The composer has used this Baroque form to create a very colorful piece that features all sections. Interesting percussion parts add to the charm of this work. *Pavana Antiqua* would be an ideal selection to program between two louder or faster pieces to show contrast in style. (© Eighth Note Publications, used by permission)

A recording of this work is available on the CD "North Winds—Canadian Wind Band Music," which may be ordered from the University of Manitoba, Faculty of Music, 65 Dafoe Road, Winnipeg, Manitoba, Canada R3T 2N2 or by calling (204) 474-9310.

FRED STRIDE (B. 1953)

FRED STRIDE TEACHES JAZZ arranging at the University of British Columbia, and is highly respected as composer, educator and arranger. Besides his many jazz compositions, he has consistently written concert music for many years for such professional ensembles as the CBC Vancouver Orchestra and the Vancouver Symphony. He has received numerous commissions and broadcasts from the CBC, and a number of his works have been released on CD by CBC Records. A recent concert work was a commission from the CBC, *Concerto for Alto Saxophone and Orchestra*, premiered by the CBC Orchestra and saxophone virtuoso Julia Nolan. In addition to directing the jazz ensemble and teaching jazz theory and arranging at the UBC School of Music, he also works as a clinician, adjudicator and teacher for festivals, camps and jazz workshops across the country.

Highlights of his past commissions include the opening and closing ceremonies of the Calgary Olympics in 1988, opening ceremonies of Expo 86, several commissions for the RCMP Band, the 1984 Papal Visit, as well as *Dialogue* written for baritone saxophone and timpani, performed by Julia Nolan for CBC. He is an associate composer of the Canadian Music Centre. (CMC and interview with the composer)

Fanfare for the Dragons
Difficulty: Grade 4
Duration: 2:33
Composed in 1991
Available from the composer (email stride@interchange.ubc.ca)

Fanfare for the Dragons was composed for the 1991 Vancouver International Dragon Boat Festival, and originally was scored for brass and percussion. This new version was completely rewritten to take advantage of the colors of the full wind band. The sound of *Fanfare For The Dragons* evokes the power and energy involved with paddling a large war canoe, or Dragon Boat. Musically speaking, the drums are front and center, playing the somewhat abstract, but no less powerful, role of master drummer for the rest of the ensemble, which is managing the paddles. The various sections come together in rhythmic unisons, representing the necessary coordination of paddlers. There are also moments when the coordination is less successful. All of this moves toward a powerful ensemble passage at the end. (Marc Crompton and interview with the composer)

This work is recorded on the CD "Trajectories" by the Pacific Symphonic Wind Ensemble, Marc Crompton, Director, and may be ordered from their website, www.pswe.ca.

Parade of the Matadors
Difficulty: Grade 4
Duration: 4:19
Composed in 2006
Available from the composer (email stride@interchange.ubc.ca)

This work originally was written for big band, and is a Spanish-styled march that conjures images of the excitement and pageantry at a bullfight. Trumpets and percussion are featured throughout, as one would expect, yet the overall effect is fresh and effective. The work retains its jazz inflections in this new arrangement, and provides opportunities to teach both march style and Spanish musical influences. (Marc Crompton and interview with the composer)

This work is recorded on the CD "Trajectories" by the Pacific Symphonic Wind Ensemble, Marc Crompton, Director, and may be ordered from their website, www.pswe.ca.

Seaquam: A Journey to the Sky
Diffficulty: Grade 4
Duration: 13:15
Composed in 1997
Available from the composer (email stride@interchange.ubc.ca)

Seaquam: A Journey to the Sky, was commissioned by Seaquam High School in Delta, BC (Jill Sparrow, band director), and presents open scoring and innovative harmonic textures. It is an imaginary journey up the Fraser River. This journey is not a real or physical journey, but one of the mind, in a phantom airship.

The first movement, *Journey and Discovery* (2:44) finds the traveler moving up the Fraser River hundreds, or even thousands, of years ago. Passing over forests the traveler comes across a long-abandoned Indian village—empty long houses, old totem poles, decaying long boats, all the signs that life once flourished for a proud people. The second movement, *Reminiscences* (6:19) is one of sadness in remembering the vibrant life that once existed in the village and is now gone. Ghostly inhabitants appear for the third movement, *Celebration and Dance* (4:22), which depicts a phantom potlatch, or celebration. The movement ends as the phantom villagers disappear into time and memory and the traveler moves on. (Marc Crompton and interview with the composer)

This work is recorded on the CD "Trajectories" by the Pacific Symphonic Wind Ensemble, Marc Crompton, Director, and may be ordered from their website, www.pswe.ca.

RAY TWOMEY (B. 1938)

CONTEMPORARY CLASSICAL MUSIC COMPOSER Ray Twomey was born in England, and moved to New Zealand after the war where he completed his schooling. He received his musical education at Victoria University of Wellington, and immigrated to Canada in 1965. He is affiliated with the Society of Composers, Authors and Music Publishers of Canada (SOCAN), an Associate Member of the Canadian Music Centre, a member of the Canadian League of Composers, the Centre for the Promotion of Contemporary Composers (CPCC), and New Zealand's SOUNZ.

Twomey has composed close to a hundred musical compositions. His portfolio includes works for symphony and chamber orchestras, concert band, opera, vocal and chamber groups, solo instruments and various choral combinations.

His music, always carefully crafted, speaks in an idiom that is both approachable and deeply personal. His musical language centers around a unique harmonic essence underlying a wonderful melodic inventiveness. The tight formal structure of his music alludes to our rich western heritage combined with the expressive freedom of the 20th century. His sonic palette is widely ranging in timbral variety while conservative in melodic content. (CMC)

General Glen: for Concert Band, Opus 26
Difficulty: Grade 3
Duration: 2:50
Composed in 2000
Available through CMC (www.musiccentre.ca)

General Glen was composed for Glen Younghusband, former Commanding Officer at Cold Lake, Alberta, and formerly Canada's Defense Attaché to Washington, DC. He was one of Canada's and NATO's youngest operational fighter pilots when, in March of 1954 at the age of nineteen, he joined 413(F) Squadron flying F-86 Sabres out of Zweibrucken, Germany. He went on to hold a number of command and staff positions in the RCAF and the Canadian Forces, including lead pilot of the Snowbirds and Commander of the 434(TAC) Fighter Squadron. He left the Forces in 1989 with the rank of Major General. (Aviation Prints, interview with the composer)

Reflections for Concert Band, Opus 24
Difficulty: Grade 3
Duration: 6:55
Composed in 1999
Available through CMC (www.musiccentre.ca)

The composer is a keen fly fisherman, and the three movements of *Reflections* were composed to celebrate the sites of his greatest fishing success stories. These stories have been known to be augmented with a modicum of embellishment from time to time, but the music is highly descriptive of the three sites. The movements are entitled: *1. Pomare Creek (12/8 time allegro); 2. Mitchell Lake (4/4 adagio);* and *3. Canmore (4/4 allegro).* (Interview with the composer)

JOHN WEINZWEIG (1913–2006)

JOHN WEINZWEIG STUDIED AT the University of Toronto, where he also founded and conducted the University of Toronto Symphony during his student years. He received a master's degree from the Eastman School of Music, where he studied composition under Bernard Rogers. While at Eastman he discovered the music of Alban Berg and the twelve-tone system, which would exert a lasting influence on his creative output. Weinzweig was the first composer in Canada to use this technique.

The composer recalls his early career: "Between the ages of 14 and 19, I studied the piano, mandolin, tuba, double bass and tenor saxophone, as well as harmony. I played and conducted school orchestras, dance bands, weddings, lodge meetings and on electioneering trucks for a range of fees between two dollars and a promise. I played *Pirates of Penzance, Poet and Peasant, Blue Danube, St. Louis Blues*, Liszt's *Hungarian Rhapsodies*, Chopin waltzes and *Tiger Rag.* At age 19 I got serious and decided to become a composer."

He continued his music studies at the University of Toronto (1934–37), where he also founded and conducted the University of Toronto Symphony during his student years. Upon the invitation of Howard Hanson he enrolled at the Eastman School of Music in Rochester, N.Y., in the Masters program, where he received his first formal guidance in composition under Bernard Rogers.

He returned to Toronto in the fall of 1938 to face the difficulties of pursuing a composing career and hostile reactions to his twelve-tone music from both musicians and members of the public. In 1941 he was invited by the CBC to compose the first original background music for dramatic radio presentations, and the following year he composed his first film score for the National Film Board of Canada. These proved to be an invaluable experience in applying his contemporary ideas to a medium that tended towards a conservative sonic background.

At the invitation of Sir Ernest MacMillan, he joined the Royal Conservatory in 1939 as teacher of composition and orchestration, and accepted a professorship at the University of Toronto in 1952, where he developed the composition department through to graduate studies. In 1978 he retired from the University as Professor Emeritus.

In 1951 Weinzweig and several of his former students, concerned by the lack of opportunities for music publication or performance of extended works, formalized their ideals and founded the Canadian League of Composers. As the League's first President, he embarked on a new career dedicated to advocating on behalf of musical creators. For many years he served on the Board of Directors of the Composers, Authors and Publishers Association of Canada (CAPAC), including as its President from 1973–75, and later on that of the amalgamated performing rights agency SOCAN. As well, he was co-planner of the Canadian Music Centre in 1959, and Chairman of the International Conference of Composers in 1960.

Richard Henninger wrote of John Weinzweig in 1973 on the occasion of his 60th birthday: "Now, at a time when mainstream twentieth century techniques are a fact of life in Canadian composition, we can look back and realize that, more than any other musician, John Weinzweig was responsible for initiating their usage. With his own music, in the early forties, Weinzweig broke the ground for the rest of us by putting sounds inspired by Berg and Stravinsky before radio and concert audiences at a time when such sounds were sure to meet resistance. By introducing contemporary techniques to a few sympathetic colleagues and students, he generated a small group of like-minded composers which became the foundation of the variety and quality found in Canadian music today." (CMC and The Canadian Encyclopedia)

Band Hut Sketches, No. 2—Parade
Difficulty: Grade 4
Duration: 4:00
Composed in 1944
Available through CMC (www.musiccentre.ca)

Band Hut Sketches No. 2 – Parade does not employ Weinzweig's customary twelve-tone writing. It is a light-textured, happy march in ABA form with important dynamic changes and interlocking lines. The B section features a piccolo solo over a chordal line, and at the end the band is portrayed as marching out of the listener's hearing, much like a patrol. The composer wrote the march for the Canadian Musical Heritage Society. (CMC and Denise Grant)

Out of the Blues
Difficulty: Grade 5
Duration: 14:00
Composed in 1981
Available through CMC (www.musiccentre.ca)

This six-movement composition was commissioned by the University of Toronto Wind Symphony through the Ontario Arts Council, and received its premiere on March 28, 1982 in MacMillan Theatre at the University of Toronto with Stephen Chenette conducting. It explores jazz and blues styles in a score characterized by light textures and exposed lines for solos, duets, trios, and other combinations of voices. There are frequent meter changes and complex rhythms, but the idea is to establish the freedom of the blues without being tied to a metronome. The movements are: *1. Deep Blues; 2. Raging Blues; 3. Meditation Blues; 4. Jumpin' Blues; 5. Meditation Blues (2)*; and *6. All Together Blues*. (CMC and Patricia Shand)

A recording of this work is available on the CD "Dreaming on the 2238," (Arbordisc UTWS 9501) by the University of Toronto Wind Symphony.

A pedagogical discussion of this work can be found on page 68 of *Guidelist of Unpublished Canadian Band Music Suitable for Student Performers* by Patricia Martin Shand.

Round Dance
Difficulty: Grade 4
Duration: 2:18
Published 1966 by Leeds
Available through CMC (www.musiccentre.ca)

A cross between a moto perpetuo and hoedown music, *Round Dance* was written in 1950 for the CBC radio talent show "Opportunity Knocks." The composer describes it as a happy piece based on a repeated theme that overlaps, such as *Frere Jacques.* This merry scherzo exemplifies many of the characteristics for which Weinzweig is known: clarity, thinness of instrumental texture and strongly rhythmic character. It begins with a brief motif that is stated first by the clarinets and then is taken up by other sections in the band until all join in a crescendo leading to the end. This piece of wit and humor was masterfully adapted for concert band by Howard Cable. (CMC and Timothy Maloney)

ELLIOT WEISGARBER (1919–2001)

COMPOSER, CLARINETIST, AND ETHNOMUSICOLOGIST Elliot Weisgarber was born in Pittsfield, Massachusetts and became a naturalized Canadian citizen in 1973. Weisgarber received his education at the Eastman School of Music, where he earned both his Bachelor of Music and Master of Music degrees as well as the Performer's Certificate in Clarinet. He studied clarinet with Rosario Mazzeo (of the Boston Symphony Orchestra) and, in New York, with Gustave Langenus; at Eastman he worked with R. Mont Arey, earning his performer's certificate. He also studied composition at Eastman with Howard Hanson and subsequently in Paris 1952–3 with Nadia Boulanger and in Los Angeles 1958–9 with Halsey Stevens. He taught at the Women's College of the University of North Carolina 1944–58 (also playing clarinet with various summer festival orchestras and many chamber music concerts in the US mid-south) and the University of California 1958–9. Weisgarber began teaching in the newly formed music department at the University of British Columbia in 1960, retiring in 1984 but retaining his association as professor emeritus. He specialized in teaching composition and Asian music. His composition pupils included Michael Conway Baker, Neil Currie, David Keeble, and Claire Lawrence and Frederick Schipizky; among his clarinet pupils was Wes Foster, who became principal clarinet of the Vancouver Symphony Orchestra in 1981.

On grants from the Canada Council Weisgarber studied Japanese music in Japan in 1966, 1967, and 1968–9 at the University of Otana and privately, becoming proficient on the shakuhachi, a traditional bamboo flute. In 1974 he toured Canada with the kotoist Miyoko Kobayashi. In 1974 he was guest speaker at the meeting of the Asian Composers' League in Kyoto, Japan, and on a second trip that year addressed the UNESCO/ISME seminar in Tokyo. In 1976 he was a guest lecturer and visiting composer at the National University of Tehran (Iran) and later that year was again a speaker for the Asian Composers' League, in Taiwan.

Weisgarber's compositional style is many-faceted, ranging from traditional works for orchestra and chamber ensemble (the latter reflecting his lifelong love of chamber music) to pieces which incorporate elements of Japanese folk music, as in *Kyoto Landscapes* for orchestra, *Japanese Miscellany* (1970) for piano, a series of chamber works for Japanese instruments, and the vocal works *Ten Japanese Folk Songs* and *Songs of a Thousand Autumns*. By the time of his death he had created a catalog of 450 compositions including chamber music, songs, orchestral works and scores for film, radio and television. (CMC, The Canadian Encyclopedia, and the composer's website, www.weisgarber.com)

Music for the Morning of the World: a Balinese Evocation
Difficulty: Grade 5
Duration: 16:00
Composed in 1977
Available through CMC (www.musiccentre.ca)

Music for the Morning of the World: A Balinese Evocation is the composer's musical impression of the island of Bali, which was given the picturesque epithet "the morning of the world" by the great Indian statesman Jawaharlal Nehru. It was written on a commission from Martin Berinbaum and the University of British Columbia Wind Symphony. The composition reflects certain aspects of gamelan music as well as Weisgarber's personal reactions to the Balinese culture, landscape, and "thoughts of the impermanence of all things."

This remarkable work is scored for a large wind ensemble plus harp, celeste, tuned gongs, and extensive percussion. The music is marked by sudden cadences and abrupt changes of dynamic and mood. Delicate percussion with high woodwinds are unexpectedly interrupted by fierce brass outbursts. Much of the harmonic content is developed from short melodic pitch sets that often appear in parallel fourths. The texture involves overlaid ostinatos of two different types. One type combines the same motives, often in the same register but rhythmically out of phase. The other type approximates the "colotonic" structure of much Indonesian music, where the same melody appears in several voices simultaneously, but the lower voices proceed rhythmically at slower speeds than the upper voices. Masterfully composed, evocative and compelling, this intriguing work places substantial demands on every member of the ensemble. (CMC, the Canadian Encyclopedia, Keith Kinder, and Martin Berinbaum)

TOM WADE WEST (B. 1960)

TOM WADE WEST TEACHES instrumental music in Toronto, Ontario, at St. George's Choir School, a school founded in the tradition of the great collegiate and cathedral choir schools in England. Outside the school, he plays first horn in the Hannaford Street Silver Band, one of Canada's most well known brass bands. He has made a number of recordings and won a JUNO Award with this ensemble. He is principal hornist in the Toronto Sinfonietta and the Oshawa-Durham Symphony Orchestra, and is also a member of the Royal Canadian Artillery Band. (© Eighth Note Music, used by permission)

Amazing Grace *with* The Last Post
Difficulty: Grade 1
Duration: 3:10
Published 2002 by Eighth Note Publications (www.enpmusic.com)

The Last Post was originally a bugle call used in British Army camps to signal the end of the day. The name derives from the practice of inspecting all the sentry posts around such a camp at the end of the day, and playing a bugle call at each of them. The "last post" was thus the last point of this inspection, and the bugle call signaling that this post had been inspected marked the end of the military day. It's now played at all Canadian military funerals (another kind of end of day) and at any Canadian ceremony honoring war dead. The parts in this arrangement for developing band are doubled to allow for varied instrumentation. It can be performed on Memorial Day, Veterans Day, or on other solemn or dignified occasions. (Keith Kinder and Eighth Note Publications, used by permission)

Nightfall in Camp: *For Solo Trumpet and Band*
Difficulty: Grade 1
Duration: 1:45
Published 2002 by Eighth Note Publications (www.enpmusic.com)

Nightfall in Camp deftly combines *The Last Post* (see above) with the hymn tune *Unto the Hills*. The band parts are well written for young players but the solo part requires a more experienced trumpeter. The solo part can also be performed by multiple players. (Fraser Linklater and Jeff Reynolds)

A recording of this work is available on the CD "North Winds—Canadian Wind Band Music," which may be ordered from the University of Manitoba, Faculty of Music, 65 Dafoe Road, Winnipeg, Manitoba, Canada R3T 2N2 or by calling (204) 474-9310.

HEALEY WILLAN (1880–1968)

HEALEY WILLAN IS ONE of the giants of Canadian music. Born in England, he moved to Toronto in 1913 to teach at the Toronto Conservatory, and quickly established himself within the musical life of the city. His reputation as a teacher was legendary; during his long career he taught an entire generation of Canadian musicians.

Admitted as an Associate of the Royal College of Organists, 1897 and Fellow, 1899, from 1903–13 he was organist and choirmaster at St. John the Baptist Kensington. He moved to Toronto in 1913 as Head of the Theory Department of the Toronto Conservatory of Music (Vice-Principal 1920–36). From 1921 until his death he was Precentor of the church of St. Mary Magdalene, Toronto, which became a mecca for church musicians. He was appointed Lecturer and Examiner for the University of Toronto in 1914. In 1934 he founded the Tudor Singers, which he conducted until 1939. In 1937 he was appointed Professor of Music at the University, a position he held until his retirement in 1950. An influential teacher, Willan was also active as the University Organist. In 1953 he was the first ever non-Briton commissioned to write an anthem for the coronation of Elizabeth II in Westminster Abbey (*O Lord Our Governour*), and in 1956 he received the Lambeth Doctorate, Mus. D. Cantaur from the Archbishop of Canterbury.

More than half of his output of over 850 compositions was sacred works for choir, which include many anthems, hymn anthems and mass settings. His secular music includes over 50 choral works, over 100 songs and song arrangements for voice and piano, many works for piano, for voice and instrumental ensemble, for voice and orchestra, two symphonies, a piano concerto, chamber works, incidental music for stage works, ballad operas and the opera *Deirdre.*

Willan was a staunch conservative, grounded in counterpoint and fugue. Although interested in new trends, he saw no reason to abandon his roots, and in *Deirdre*, which he regarded as one of his finest works, he centered on a post-Wagnerian idiom. His choral music composed for St. Mary Magdalene has had a significant influence on composers of all denominations. His major works signaled the acceptance in Canada of large-scale composition. Frequently known as the "Dean of Canadian Composers," he was made a Companion of the Order of Canada, his country's highest civilian honor, at its inception in 1967. (CMC, The Canadian Encyclopedia, and The Order of Canada)

Elegie Heroique
Difficulty: Grade 4
Duration: 4:00
Published 1971 by Boosey and Hawkes (out of print)
Scored by William Atkins

This elegant ceremonial march was written for the 100th anniversary of the Queen's Own Rifles of Canada, a militia regiment based in Toronto. The Queen's

Own Rifles Band premiered it in 1960. Typical of Willan's conservative compositional style, this work is very tonal and reminiscent of Elgar and of Walton's *Crown Imperial* but not as demanding. The major portion is written in D flat, and the coda in B flat. The opening fanfare is the basis for linkage between the three main sections, and recurs at the end. Like Willan's *Royce Hall Suite*, this work was scored by someone else: in this case, the conductor of the Queen's Own Rifles, William Atkins. (CMC and Timothy Maloney)

A recording of this work is available on the CD "Concert in the Park," disk number SMCD5079, by the Edmonton Wind Ensemble, and may be ordered from the Canadian Music Centre (www.musiccentre.ca). A recording of this work also is available on the CD "A Lakeshore Concert," by the Lakeshore Concert Band of Montreal, and may be ordered by emailing the band at *lakeshoreconcertband@coolgoose.com*.

Royce Hall Suite
Difficulty: Grade 4
Duration: 10:00
Published 1952 by Associated Music (out of print)
Edited by William Teague

During the summer of 1949, when Willan was a visiting professor at the University of California, Los Angeles, the band director at UCLA, Patton McNaughton, asked him for a band piece. Willan named his new composition *Royce Hall Suite*, after the band hall on the UCLA campus. Perhaps because of Willan's unfamiliarity with the band medium, William Teague, a staff arranger for BMI, scored the composition. *Royce Hall Suite* is a landmark composition in Canadian repertoire. Conservative in form, the suite reflects Willan's philosophy that he should "add to the beauty of the past…rather than search out the shape and sound of things to come."

The first movement, *Prelude and Fugue*, reflects the organ works of Bach and Handel that Willan knew so well as an ecclesiastical organist. The second, *Menuet*, is light and restrained, and evokes the harmoniemusic of the 18th century; and the third, *Rondo*, appears at first to be a typical march, except that the primary melody is eleven bars long with unusual phrasing throughout. Much of the excitement of the piece lies in its creative scoring, such as highly effective harmony that freely blends tonal and modal elements, and in unconventional phrasing. The rich brass and woodwind sections are reminiscent of the music of Walton and Bax. Although out of print, it may still be found in larger and well-established libraries, and would be well worth the search. (CMC, Keith Kinder and Timothy Maloney)

A recording of this work is available on the CD "Dreaming on the 2238," (Arbordisc UTWS 9501) by the University of Toronto Wind Symphony.

MAX WILLIAMS (B. 1963)

MAX WILLIAMS RECEIVED HIS Bachelor of Music in trombone performance from Northwestern University (Chicago). He studied trombone with Frank Crisafulli and conducting with John P. Paynter and Frederick Ockwell, and was a frequent substitute and extra player with the Chicago Symphony and Pops orchestras. He also was a member of the Civic Orchestra of Chicago for four years. Mr. Williams continued his music training in Canada with the Royal Conservatory Orchestra and the National Youth Orchestra of Canada. He holds a Bachelor of Education degree from the University of Western Ontario, and has been teaching music at both the elementary and secondary level for the past 12 years. Mr. Williams remains active as a professional performer and composer/arranger. (© Eighth Note Publications, used by permission)

Eagle Pass
Difficulty: Grade 3
Duration: 5:20
Published 2002 by Eighth Note Publications (www.enpmusic.com)

Craigellachie!, a Scottish battle cry, is the name given to the spot near Eagle Pass, which cuts through Canada's Rocky Mountains, where, on November 7, 1885, Donald Smith drove the last spike of the Trans-Canada Railway into the earth. This piece is an attempt to express musically the indomitable spirit of all those thousands who struggled so hard to build not a railway, but a nation. (The Canadian Encyclopedia and Eighth Note Publications, used by permission)

The Plains of Pangaea
Difficulty: Grade 4
Duration: 7:05
Published 2004 by Eighth Note Publications (www.enpmusic.com)

225 million years ago, all of the earth's landmasses were joined together into one super continent, Pangaea, surrounded by a single universal sea, Panthalassa. This giant land was inhabited by creatures totally alien to the world we know. This dramatic work is an attempt to capture, in music, the experience of voyaging to The Plains of Pangaea, and features creative combinations of instruments and tone colors. (© Eighth Note Publications, used by permission)

Two Native Legends
Difficulty: Grade 4
Duration: 8:50
Published 2002 by Eighth Note Publications (www.enpmusic.com)

This dramatic work is based on the legends "The Fairy Ring" from the Chippewa tribe and "The Witch of the Mitche-hant" from the Passamaquoddy. The first legend tells of the circular pathways that the Chippewa found on the prairie, worn as if by the tread of many feet. The second tells of a young hunter who fell in love with a beautiful maiden in the forest who was actually a ghost. Both sections contain evocative writing for both winds and percussion. (© Eighth Note Publications, used by permission)

JOHN WILSON (B. 1958)

BORN AND RAISED IN Bowmanville, Ontario, John Wilson studied writing and arranging in his music degree studies at the University of Toronto, as well as with Boss Brass member Ian McDougall. A multi-talented musician, Wilson holds a degree in trombone performance from the University of Toronto, and has experience in both the classical and jazz idioms. Wilson's first arrangement for concert band, *The Huron Carol*, has become a popular Canadian concert selection during the Christmas season.

In addition to his compositions for concert band, Wilson's work includes original pieces and arrangements for stage band and trombone choir. (© Northdale Music Press, used by permission)

Commonwealth March: Officer's Processional
Difficulty: Grade 4
Duration: 3:15
Published 1996 by Northdale Music Press (www.northdalemusic.com)

Commonwealth March: Officers' Processional debuted in grand circumstance. It was originally titled *Fanfare and Processional* but was officially retitled when Music Director Ian McDougall used the melody to open the 1994 Commonwealth Games in Victoria, British Columbia. As the featured piece of the opening ceremonies of the Games, *Commonwealth March* was heard by a live audience of over 50,000 and an estimated television audience of 500,000,000. Prince Edward was among the dignitaries who entered the stadium to this stately but lively processional.

The composition begins with a brass fanfare followed by a dignified, tuneful melody, with jazz-based harmonies, carried by the clarinet section. The middle section and the trio that follows can be repeated if necessary for commencement activities and convocations. The trio features a trumpet solo and a quirky surprise played by the piccolo. The piece finishes in the coda with another fanfare flourish by the brass. (© Northdale Music Press, used by permission)

The Huron Carol
Difficulty: Grade 4
Duration: 3:30
Published 1993 by Northdale Music Press (www.northdalemusic.com)

Having arrived in New France in 1615, the early Roman Catholic missionaries proceeded to establish a presence near Midland, Ontario. They translated new and traditional religious texts into native languages, often adding musical accompaniment. One such work—now popularly known as the first Canadian Christmas carol—is *The Huron Carol*, or *Jesous Ahatonhia (Jesus is Born)*. This composition is widely believed to have been adapted from a 16th century folk song *Une jeune pucelle (The Young Flea)* in the mid-1600s for the Hurons at Ste. Marie, by the Jesuit missionary Jean de Brébeuf.

Although part of an oral tradition for almost 100 years, it was not until the 18th century that the music was written down by Fr. de Villeneuve, a Jesuit priest. First published in Noëls anciens de la Nouvelle-France in 1907 by Ernest Myrand, it has since been variously adapted for voice, piano, choir, and orchestra. It is the subject of the 1977 Canadian postage stamp Christmas series and an NFB filmstrip: *Huron Indian Christmas Carol*.

The Huron Carol is familiar in the minds of many as Christmas music of identifiably Canadian origin. The composer has not changed the traditional minor-key melody, but rather has made interesting use of contemporary harmonies, transforming the piece through the use of altered dominant chords adapted from the repertoire of the jazz tradition. The simple minor melody lends itself well to close-voiced modal harmony. (© Northdale Music Press, used by permission)

GERHARD WUENSCH (1925–2007)

GERHARD WUENSCH WAS BORN in Austria. After receiving a Doctor of Philosophy from the University of Vienna in 1950, and a diploma in composition and piano from the State Academy of Music in Vienna in 1952, he continued his studies in theory with Paul Pisk at the University of Texas. He then went on to teach at Butler University in Indiana from 1956–63.

In Canada since 1964, he held positions at the University of Toronto from 1964–69 and at the University of Calgary from 1969–73, before becoming Professor of theory and composition at the University of Western Ontario. There he met his wife, Jean Anderson, an accomplished musician and composer in her own right, who was teaching at UWO.

Wuensch's musical convictions were simple ones: " I always try to write music which is accessible to the widest possible audience, reasonably well crafted and economical, in that it requires a minimum of rehearsal time. By today's standards of 'New Music,' my style is hopelessly outdated. I have even been known to employ key signatures occasionally. Music critics tend to dismiss my music outright, while other composers at best tolerate it with a condescending smile." (CMC and Jean Anderson Wuensch)

Six Guises
Difficulty: Grade 6
Duration: 22:50
Composed 1972
Available through CMC (www.musiccentre.ca)

Six Guises was commissioned by Keith Campbell MacMillan, head of the Canadian Music Centre in 1972 for "Showcase" a non-competitive festival of contemporary music that is held every two years in Toronto. *Six Guises* is an exploration of various compositional techniques with narration written by Wuensch's friend MacMillan, who was the son of Sir Ernest MacMillan. A short introduction is followed by a theme and six variations, each one demonstrating a different compositional style. The movements are: *Introduction - The tune - Disguise I: traditional harmony - Disguise II: modal harmony - Disguise III: Polytonality - Disguise IV: Variable meters - Disguise V: Twelve-tone - and Disguise VI: Finale.* This is a challenging work in every respect, but an excellent example of each compositional style. (CMC, Patricia Martin Shand, and Jean Anderson Wuensch)

A pedagogical discussion of this work can be found on page 69 of *Guidelist of Unpublished Canadian Band Music Suitable for Student Performers* by Patricia Martin Shand.

INDEX BY COMPOSER

Lloyd Burritt

Grade 4
Crystal Earth (1987-1992)

Grade 5
Gabriola Gambol for Symphonic Winds
Passage Island

Howard Cable

Grade 2
Scene in Iqualuit

Grade 3
Berczy Portraits
Marchmanship

Grade 3.5
Saskatchewan Overture

Grade 4
The Banks of Newfoundland
Fiat Lux
Good Medicine-A Charlie Russell Suite
Hard Oil
McIntyre Ranch Country
O Canada

Grade 5
Newfoundland Rhapsody
Ontario Pictures
Quebec Folk Fantasy
Scottish Rhapsody
Snake Fence Country: a rural holiday

Grade 6
Stratford Suite: Four Shakespearean Scenes for
   Concert Band

Morley Calvert

Grade 4
Romantic Variations
Suite on Canadian Folk Songs

Bruce Carlson

Grade 3
Toledo

Chan Ka Nin

Grade 5
Ecstacy

Grade 6
Momento Mori

Stephen Chatman

Grade 2
Grouse Mountain Lullaby

Grade 3
Mountain Sojourn
Walnut Grove Suite

Donald Coakley

Grade 1
Land of the Silver Birch
Regal Salute

Grade 1.5
Suite for a Band of Players

Grade 2
Donkey Riding
Gentle Clouds Roll By—A Chippewa Lullaby
Songs for the Morning Band
Suite for a Band of Players
The Twentieth Century Band

Grade 3
Bonavist Harbour
Bright Blue Water
Celebration
Elegaic Motives
The Garnet and the Gold
Lyric Essay
The Moon Reflected in Twin Ponds
Now the Morning is Begun
Prelude on a Festive Hymn Tune

Grade 3.5
A Distant Voice

Grade 4
Antiphonals
A Canadian Folk Rhapsody
Cantos
Canzona
Jubilant Dialogue
Masquerade
Toccata Festiva

Grade 3
Galactic March
Newfoundland Folk Song
Petty Harbour Bait Skiff
A Seaside Ballad
Terra Nova Overture

Brent Dutton

Grade 6
Patrician Dances
Symphony No. 5: Dark Spirals

Malcolm Forsyth

Grade 5
Colour Wheel

Grade 6
Kaleidoscope

Harry Freedman

Grade 2
A la Claire Fontaine

Grade 4
Laurentian Moods

Grade 6
Sonata for Wind Orchestra

Vince Gassi

Grade 3
Ships With Sails Unfurled

James McDonald Gayfer

Grade 3
Canadian Landscape

Grade 4
Royal Visit
The Wells of Marah

Alan Gilliland

Grade 3
Dreamscapes

Derek Healey

Grade 6
One Mid-Summer's Morning: An English Set
    for Wind Band

John Herberman

Grade 3
Couchiching Suite

Grade 4
The Fisher Who Died in His Bed

Godfrey Ridout

Grade 3
Partita Accademica

Grade 4
Tafelmusik

Sid Robinovitch

Grade 3
Sphinx

Grade 4
West of Bali

Nicole Rodrigue

Grade 5
Désastre

Ronald Royer

Grade 4
Overture to an Unscripted Movie

Jeffrey Ryan

Grade 3
Orillia Panorama

Thomas Schudel

Grade 5
Elegy and Exaltation

Grade 6
Triptych

Norman Sherman

Grade 4
The Pioneers: suite for band

Jack Sirulnikoff

Grade 3
Nova Scotia Fantasy
Variations on a Rollicking Tune

Anita Sleeman

Grade 4
Bouree Variations
Carol of the Bells: A Fantasy on the Christmas
    Carol

Grade 5
Cantus
Celebration Overture
Quetzalcoatl

Grade 6
Cryptic Variations

Jeff Smallman

Grade 1
Coming Home

Grade 2
And Birds Will Sing Again
Pavana Antiqua

Grade 3
Grand Procession
Shades of Majesty

Grade 4
Arkhangelsk

Grade 5
Sinfonietta

Fred Stride

Grade 4
Fanfare for the Dragons
Parade of the Matadors
Seaquam: A Journey to the Sky

Ray Twomey

Grade 3
General Glen: for Concert Band, Opus 26
Reflections for Concert Band, Opus 2

John Weinzweig

Grade 4
Band Hut Sketches, No. 2 – Parade
Round Dance

Grade 5
Out of the Blues

Elliot Weisgarber

Grade 5
Music for the Morning of the World: a Balinese
    Evocation

Tom Wade West

Grade 1
Amazing Grace with The Last Post
Nightfall in Camp

Healey Willan

Grade 4
Elegie Heroique
Royce Hall Suite

Max Williams

Grade 3
Eagle Pass

Grade 4
The Plains of Pangaea
Two Native Legends

INDEX BY GRADE

Grade 1

Amazing Grace with The Last Post	Tom Wade West
Apache Lullaby	Michael Colgrass
Coming Home	Jeff Smallman
A French Canadian Suite	Arnold MacLaughlan
Land of the Silver Birch	Donald Coakley
Land of the Silver Birch	Douglas Court
Nightfall in Camp	Tom Wade West
O Canada	David Marlatt
Reesor Park	David Marlatt
Regal Salute	Donald Coakley
Suite for a Band of Players	Donald Coakley
Wedgewood Festival	Douglas Court
Woodcrest Overture	David Marlatt

Grade 2

A la Claire Fontaine	Harry Freedman
And Birds Will Sing Again	Jeff Smallman
Cape St. Mary's	Jim Duff
Celtic Dance	Douglas Court
Concord Fanfare	David Marlatt
Crimond	David Marlatt
Daydreams	Andre Jutras
Donkey Riding	Donald Coakley
Gentle Clouds Roll By - A Chippewa Lullaby	Donald Coakley
Greenwood Overture	Jim Duff
Grouse Mountain Lullaby	Stephen Chatman
Jim	Ron MacKay
Journey to a New World	Douglas Court
Kawartha Legend	Douglas Court
March and Interlude	Jim Duff
Markham Fair Suite	David Marlatt
O Canada	David Marlatt
Old Churches	Michael Colgrass
Pavana Antiqua	Jeff Smallman
Scene in Iqaluit	Howard Cable
Songs for the Morning Band	Donald Coakley
Suite for a Band of Players	Donald Coakley
True North	Douglas Court
The Twentieth Century Band	Donald Coakley
Two Pieces for Band	Gary Kulesha

Grade 3

Grade 4

Grade 4 (continued)

Moventa	Andre Jutras
Night Is No Longer Summer Soft	Murray Adaskin
O Canada	Howard Cable
Overture to an Unscripted Movie	Ronald Royer
Pacifica	Bob Buckley
Parade of the Matadors	Fred Stride
The Pioneers: suite for band	Norman Sherman
The Plains of Pangaea	Max Williams
Romantic Variations	Morley Calvert
Round Dance	John Weinzweig
Royal Visit	James McDonald Gayfer
Royce Hall Suite	Healey Willan
Sanctus (for Symphonic Band)	Robert Bauer
Seaquam: A Journey to the Sky	Fred Stride
Shadow Play	Bob Buckley
Suite on Canadian Folk Songs	Morley Calvert
Tafelmusik	Godfrey Ridout
Theme from "ReBoot"	Bob Buckley
Toccata Festiva	Donald Coakley
Two Native Legends	Max Williams
Tyendinaga: Legend for concert band	Clifford Crawley
The Wells of Marah	James McDonald Gayfer
West of Bali	Sid Robinovitch

Grade 5

100 Years of Fanfares	Elizabeth Raum
Canadian Folk Song Fantasy	William McCauley
Cantus	Anita Sleeman
Celebration Overture	Anita Sleeman
Chanson Joyeuse	Michael Conway Baker
Chorale - Homage Anton Bruckner	Michael Parker
Colour Wheel	Malcolm Forsyth
The Cremation of Sam McGee	Michael Purves-Smith
Desastre	Nicole Rodrigue
Ecstasy	Chan Ka Nin
Elegy and Exaltation	Thomas Schudel
Ensembles for Winds	Gary Kulesha
Gabriola Gambol for Symphonic Winds	Lloyd Burritt
Glorious 100th	Louis Applebaum
Hannaford Overture	J. Scott Irvine
High Spirits	Louis Applebaum
Landscapes: Opus 59, for band	Michael Parker
May-Day	Clifford Crawley
Music for the Morning of the World	Elliot Weisgarber

APPENDIX 1: FOUR YEAR PLANS

The following lists in grades 1 through 6 are my suggestions for a four-year cycle of works at each level of difficulty for a director who might wish to focus on Canadian band literature with his or her band. These lists are only a starting point, but I hope you will find them intriguing and helpful.

	Grade 1	Grade 2
Year 1	David Marlatt *Reesor Park* Michael Colgrass *Apache Lullaby* Douglas Court *Wedgewood Festival*	Donald Coakley *Donkey Riding* Michael Colgrass *Old Churches* Gary Kulesha *Two Pieces for Band* Stephen Chatman *Grouse Mountain Lullaby*
Year 2	Arnold MacLaughlan *A French-Canadian Suite* Douglas Court *Land of the Silver Birch* Donald Coakley *Regal Salute*	Jeff Smallman *Pavana Antiqua* Harry Freedman *A la Claire Fontaine* Jim Duff *Greenwood Overture* Douglas Court *Kawartha Legend*
Year 3	Tom Wade West *Amazing Grace with The Last Post* Donald Coakley *Suite for a Band of Players* Jeff Smallman *Coming Home*	Donald Coakley *Songs for the Morning Band* Ron MacKay *Jim* Andre Jutras *Daydreams* Howard Cable *Scene in Iqaluit*
Year 4	Tom Wade West *Nightfall in Camp* David Marlatt *Woodcrest Overture*	David Marlatt *Markham Fair Suite* Douglas Court *True North* Donald Coakley *Gentle Clouds Roll By: A Chippewa Lullaby* Jim Duff *March and Interlude*

	Grade 3	Grade 4
Year 1	Jim Duff *Newfoundland Folk Song or A Seaside Ballad* Stephen Chatman *Mountain Sojourn* Michael Conway Baker *The Mountains* William A. Mighton *Fields of Honour*	John Herberman *The Fisher Who Died in His Bed* Godfrey Ridout *Tafelmusik* Healey Willan *Royce Hall Suite (out of print)* Donald Coakley *Toccata Festiva*
Year 2	Howard Cable *Berczy Portraits or Saskatchewan Overture* Bruce Carlson *Toledo* Andre Jutras *They Came Sailing* Donald Coakley *Lyric Essay*	Allan Bell *From Chaos to the Birth of a Dancing Star* Sid Robinovitch *West of Bali* Clifford Crawley *Tyendinaga: Legend for Concert Band* Howard Cable *Good Medicine—A Charlie Russell Suite*
Year 3	James McDonald Gayfer *Canadian Landscape* Allan Bell *In the Eye of the Four Winds* Scott Macmillan *Cheticamp Overture* Gary Kulesha *March in F*	Healey Willan *Elegie Heroique (out of print)* Donald Coakley *Masquerade* Fred Stride *Seaquam: A Journey to the Sky* Murray Adaskin *Night Is No Longer Summer Soft*
Year 4	Jack Sirulnikoff *Nova Scotia Fantasy* John Herberman *Couchiching Suite* Elizabeth Raum *Sodbuster* Vince Gassi *Ships With Sails Unfurled*	Anita Sleeman *Carol of the Bells* Morley Calvert *Suite on Canadian Folk Songs* Bob Buckley *Pacifica* Harry Freedman *Laurentian Moods*

	Grade 5	Grade 6
Year 1	Michael Conway Baker *Chanson Joyeuse* Louis Applebaum *Suite of Miniature Dances* Chan Ka Nin *Ecstasy* Elizabeth Raum *100 Years of Fanfares*	Donald Coakley *Sonics* Malcolm Forsyth *Kaleidoscope* Brent Dutton *Symphony No 5: Dark Spirals*
Year 2	Lloyd Burritt *Gabriola Gambol* Howard Cable *Ontario Pictures* Phil Nimmons *Riverscape* J. Scott Irvine *Hannaford Overture*	Michael Colgrass *Arctic Dreams* Chan Ka Nin *Momento Mori* Howard Cable *Stratford Suite* Anita Sleeman *Cryptic Variations*
Year 3	Pierre Mercure *Pantomime* Walter Buczynski *The Trilogy of the 2238* Malcolm Forsyth *Colour Wheel* Phil Nimmons *Skyscape: Sleeping Beauty and the Lions*	Gerhard Wuensch *Six Guises* Harry Freedman *Sonata for Wind Orchestra* Derek Healey *One Midsummer's Morning* Brent Dutton *Patrician Dances*
Year 4	John Weinzweig *Out of the Blues* Donald Coakley *Vive la Canadienne* Thomas Schudel *Elegy and Exaltation* William McCauley *Canadian Folk Song Fantasy*	Thomas Schudel *Tryptich* Donald Coakley *Declarative Statements* Michael Colgrass *The Winds of Nagual* Robert Lemay *Apeldoorm, Nederland*

About the Author

Michael Burch-Pesses is Director of Bands at Pacific University in Forest Grove, Oregon, where he conducts the Wind Ensemble, Jazz Band, and Jazz Choir, and teaches courses in conducting and music education. He holds Master of Music and Doctor of Musical Arts degrees in conducting from the Catholic University of America in Washington, DC. Since coming to Pacific University in 1995 he received the Junior Faculty Award (1998) and was named a Wye Fellow of the Aspen Institute (1999). In 2006 he received the S.S. Johnson Foundation Award for Excellence in Teaching and the Citation of Excellence from the National Band Association. He is listed in Who's Who in America and Who's Who in American Education.

He enjoyed a distinguished career as a bandmaster in the United States Navy before arriving at Pacific University, enlisting as a hornist and working his way up through the ranks to become the Navy's senior bandmaster and Head of the Navy Music Program. During his Navy career he served as Leader of the Naval Academy Band in Annapolis, Maryland. Under his direction the Naval Academy Band received the George Howard Citation of Musical Excellence from the John Philip Sousa Foundation, the highest civilian award for a military band. He also served as Assistant Leader of the Navy Band in Washington, DC, and Director of the Commodores, the Navy's official jazz ensemble.

An internationally active adjudicator, lecturer and clinician, he has conducted throughout the United States, Canada, South America, Europe, Asia, and Australia. In 2000 he conducted the British Columbia All-Province Honour Band, and in 2002 he adjudicated the National Concert Band Festival of New Zealand.

Dr. Burch-Pesses also is the Conductor and Musical Director of the Oregon Symphonic Band, Oregon's premier adult band. The Oregon Symphonic Band is composed primarily of musicians from the Portland/Vancouver area. Men and women of many professions are represented in the ensemble, which performs three concert series annually and has appeared in concert at numerous state, regional, and international music conferences, including the All-Northwest MENC conference, the Western International Band Clinic, and the prestigious Midwest Clinic in Chicago.

His professional affiliations include the Oregon Music Educators Association, Music Educators National Conference, National Band Association, and Oregon Band Directors Association. He is the president-elect of the Northwest Division of the College Band Directors National Association, and a charter member of the Oregon chapter of Phi Beta Mu.